Boss Talk

Boss
Talk

*Top CEOs Share
the Ideas
That Drive the
World's Most
Successful
Companies*

THE EDITORS OF
The Wall
Street Journal

INTRODUCTION BY
TOM PETERS

RANDOM HOUSE
TRADE PAPERBACKS
New York

Library of Congress Cataloging-in-Publications Data

Boss talk : top CEOs share the ideas that drive the
world's most successful companies /
by the editors of the Wall Street Journal ;
introduction by Tom Peters.
p. cm.
ISBN 0-375-75885-2
1. Chief executive officers—Interviews. 2. Industrial
management. I. Wall Street journal.
HD38.2 .B67 2002
658.4'—dc21   2001041756

Random House website address: www.atrandom.com

Printed in the United States of America
on acid-free paper

2   4   6   8   9   7   5   3

First Trade Paperback Edition

Book design by Jennifer Ann Daddio

Contents

Part Three: Building a Brand

Part Four: Learning from the New Economy

Part Five: Trendspotting

Part Six: Beating the Competition

Part Seven: Leading a Successful Turnaround or Transition

Introduction
Tom Peters

A few years back I wrote a book called *The Pursuit of Wow*.

Well . . . forget *that*.

There's no "wow" here.

That is, this is better than "wow."

Boss Talk is just that: conversations with an extraordinary set of "bosses." And what they have to tell us is . . .

Mundane. (Read: common sense.)

Inspiring. (Read: *un*common sense.)

Hence my Highlights Tape from this remarkable book.

Consider Jack Welch. Arguably, he did better than almost anybody running a business during the last hundred years or so. Yet he tells us that his real secret is . . . no secret at all. Rather, it's simply an abiding obsession with developing talent (an idea worthy of the best National Football League general manager). Moreover, he insists—despite the astonishing size of GE—that his executives think of themselves as running a grocery store. They'll instinctively make the correct decisions, he claims, if they focus on the basics of people and customers and service and innovation. Could it be that "simple" (hard, really, if you've ever run a grocery store)?

To some extent, yes. That's the "secret" of this book: a focus on—nay, obsession with—the basics, within the context of the particular enterprise.

Microsoft CEO Steve Ballmer also offers us simplicity itself. He insists that the Big Guy at Big Co. has to proffer a crystal-clear definition of where True North is. The endpoint must also be exciting enough to stir thousands to uncommon effort. "Clear thought" and "leading proposition" are the terms he uses. It's boss-as-weathervane. Then, the Big Guy must signal the staff about what really matters . . . and thus, by definition, what *doesn't*. (As a CEO friend said to me, "Remember, Tom, it's the 'To don'ts' that really matter." Amen.)

Nice, Steve. (And—the point of all this—such clarity is absent in nine of ten big enterprises.)

While the market has gone bonkers on him, it would be absurd to denigrate the amazing track record that John Chambers has put together at Cisco Systems. Yes, he's developed a brilliant strategy of *acquiring* innovation. (Some question it. I'm not one of them. I applaud.) But his secret isn't "cool acquisitions." It's getting mileage out of those acquisitions, in a world where most efforts at combination—small and large—fail, by far, to live up to their potential. Thus, from Brother Chambers we hear about . . . guess what . . . talent. (Welch redux.) In particular, we hear about developing and maintaining an energetic corporate culture in the face of incredible growth—which excites the entrepreneurial sorts Chambers has bought/brought to the party.

Chambers also makes an impassioned plea for putting customers first. It's like the "talent thing." That is, putting customers *really first* in every corporate decision and process— miles and miles beyond typical King Customer lip service. Note: *Chambers claims he's repeatedly amazed that, upon spending time with the senior leadership of big companies, he hears literally nothing, in the space of several hours, directly about the customer.* That ain't Cisco. That ain't Chambers.

How boring, eh? Not.

While there have been numerous hiccups along the way, Daimler Chrysler CEO Juergen Schrempp has done a better than decent job with a monstrously difficult merger. And he too offers us . . . ho-hum . . . simplicity itself.

Well, it's simplicity in retrospect—but quite counterintuitive until one gives it a second, and then third, thought. Schrempp claims that he coined the phrase "the danger of a deadly wish for harmony." That is, he contends that most post-merger marriages fail because everybody tries to "income average," in effect, to push off the hard decisions and offer hopelessly political compromises. Schrempp also calls these all-important, make-or-break decisions "digital decisions." That is, one or zero. A clear yes. Or a clear no.

And don't wobble! Get on with it! He argues persuasively that making a decision and moving forward, and seeing what happens, even if it's messy, is far better than endless debate followed by mealymouthed compromise. A damn good point, I'd aver.

The Schrempp Doctrine is followed by the thoughts of per-haps the most successful Merger Master of them all in recent times, Sandy Weill, who put together Citicorp and Travelers. Weill tells us—*again*—that *success flows from moving damned fast* and then getting on with the next chapter, as opposed to leaving thousands (hundreds of thousands, in his case) in the dark about what's up. Speedy and decisive decision-making, he claims, is the key to holding on to good people and getting the great mass of individuals focused on the future—rather than allowing them to wallow in the turmoil of bent relationships that inevitably accompany a merger. He also underscores another obvious point, which many others fudge on: Treating the acquired company with the utmost respect is a sine qua non of merger-integration success.

Then Novartis CEO Daniel Vasella chimes in on the topic of mergers and rapid growth. And what he gives us, in effect, is "ditto Welch." It's all about developing the Very Best Talent Pool. (Obvious, yes. But worth repeating. Again, again, and then again. Which so many of these CEOs do.) *It's the talent, stupid!* No one ever claims not to be a "people person." But few can match the obsession—and "obsession" is exactly the right word—of people like Vasella and Welch and Ballmer. An obsession with Talent. Which occupies most of your (very long) days.

Vasella adds, intriguingly, that when you acquire something big, you must immediately figure out how to break it up and, then, create energetic, forward-looking business units that take advantage of overall size while avoiding the sluggishness accompanying the "huge complexities" that invariably attend to huge organizations.

Amen, redux.

And now: more basics. But this time on the topic of brand building. Basics from someone who's most famous for creating amazing "buzz." Namely, Tina Brown, currently chairman and editor in chief of *Talk* magazine (and formerly Turnaround Queen at *Vanity Fair* and *The New Yorker*). Brown gives lots of useful tips, but the one that I like best is again worthy of repeating time and time again: *There's no such thing as "buzz" that works . . . unless the product is Seriously Cool.* Yes, Brown is a born buzzmeister, but a buzzmeister who first and foremost created one hell of a product—significantly different and more energetic than what she inherited.

She also reveals a confidence that I suspect is essential to those determined to keep an enterprise, media or nonmedia, perpetually fresh. She insists she's "easily bored." While that speaks to freshness, Brown paradoxically also champions consistency: "I have always felt that you should be able to throw a magazine on the floor at any page, and know whose magazine it is." Whoops! We've just been let in on the Great Secret of Brand Power: *fresh and familiar at once.*

Ms. Brown's theme is echoed and amplified by Kevin Roberts, the chief executive of Saatchi & Saatchi. The secret of brand building is no secret at all. The advertising man says, in effect: It ain't about the advertising. It's about how incredibly exciting the product is and the degree to which it works its long-term emotional appeal on us. For example, he claims that "Apple is the most sensual product since the vibrator." And he chuckles about how his daughter "almost strokes" her new Volkswagen Beetle. Branding, then, for these two masters, is not skin deep: It's soul deep.

Michael Dell provides brilliant lessons from the new economy. And simple ones. (Though these require a mighty effort—as do all these "simple" ideas—to execute.) Dell, of course, is the unparalleled Master of the Supply Chain. He's driven. Obsessed. Driven by his effort to shrink/eliminate "transaction costs" (think of them as friction) throughout the entire Dell system, from supplier to customer. It's not about "working over the supply chain." It's about a complete reconception of a perfectly oiled supply chain—doing the most incredibly complex tasks at, literally, the speed of light. Dell's newest plant, for instance, turns out twenty thousand custom-engineered computers a day, and yet needs only one hundred square feet of spare-parts storage. (Holy smokes!) Again, in the Michael Dell interview, *one is repeatedly struck by the absolute clarity and intensity of his vision.*

Eaton Corp. was founded in 1911 as an axle maker for trucks. Yet Eaton CEO Stephen Hardis has the company rockin' in the new economy. The secret of his success, above all, flies in the face of one of the relatively new tenets of management wisdom, developed during the last two decades. There can indeed be too much of a good thing, per Hardis. Namely, you can do too much refinement, too much continuous improvement, add too many new features that are exciting to the insider but relatively useless to the customer. Hence his plea that you shouldn't "have your resources trapped in areas that are inherently zero-sum gains with a very marginal return." Instead, he argues that one must step boldly into new fields, developing new strengths that allow you to add significant value.

Hardis also emphasizes a theme that Ballmer and several others underscore: keeping oneself fresh. He says he's blessed by having been a liberal-arts major, and he continues to read and attend a wide variety of events—frequently learning something quirky that leads to a significant strategic breakthrough for his fundamentally conservative company. Hmmmmm.

Amazon founder and CEO Jeff Bezos is another one of those speed fanatics. He insists that the initial product—even the one in the marketplace that the customer sees—doesn't need to be perfect. It needs to be *there.* Fast. Now. "I'm often encouraging people to go faster, even if it means a worse initial product," he says. "I want us to start learning." Then, using the extraordinary customer feedback rituals that Amazon has pioneered, you do it over and over . . . and then over again . . . until you turn it into something fabulous.

Sounding Welchian, Bezos also talks at length about the imperative of talent development in a very fast growing company. One intriguing—*basic!*—point he emphasizes is the ability of an exec to demonstrate how good he or she has been at hiring in the past. "When I'm interviewing a senior job candidate," he reports, "my biggest worry is how good they are at hiring. I spend at least half the interview on that."

In this nutty, crazy world—which is only getting nuttier and crazier in so many dimensions—Bezos also underscores, Hardis-like, the need to refresh. (Call it the Busy Person's Refreshment Imperative.) "It's easy to let the in-box side of your life overwhelm you," he says, "so you become a totally reactive person. The only remedy I know of is to set aside some fraction of your time as your own." Hence Bezos religiously uses Tuesdays and Thursdays as "my proactive days, when I try not to schedule meetings." Tough to do. Demands incredible discipline. And, if done, a brilliant practice. Theme redux: Simple (in concept). Tough (in practice).

No CEO has to make bigger bets on the (uncertain) future than Boeing chairman Phil Condit. He provides lots of sage advice, but the centerpiece for me is his strong assertion that "just doing what your competitor does is probably the biggest opportunity to lose money." As an example, he refers to Douglas and Lockheed, who "both built tri-jets [in the 1960s] to the identical specs, and just beat each other silly."

All I want to do is tell a dozen CEOs I know, "Listen to this guy! Same old same-old is a design for unmitigated disaster."

Repetition: It's an author's no-no. And there's plenty of it here. Except that repetition is the very strength of this book. On the topic of turnarounds and succession, for example, former Federal-Mogul Corporation chairman Robert Miller tells us that the secret in tough times is: Tell everybody the truth. (The truth: That's a hell of an insight. Honored in the breach by 90 percent of turnaround and merger execs, in my experience. Tell the truth. Amen, Brother Miller.) Miller also reinforces the notion that in stressful times, speed matters. A lot. I.e.: Do something. Get moving. Exude a sense of motion and momentum. And then Miller caps it by making a plea almost as strong as John Chambers's at Cisco Systems for listening to the customers!

Miller dogma: Rule #1: Play it straight. Rule #2: You need to make decisions. Don't study things to death. Most of the things that really need to be done will be plainly obvious. Rule #3: Listen to the customer. Your customers are usually more perceptive than you are about what you need to do with your company.

Nice.

What a tough pair of acts to follow. Lee Scott had to follow David Glass, who had to follow Sam Walton. Scott is the CEO of Wal-Mart. He provides numerous insights, but the one I like best is another of those common refrains in this book. "The biggest mistake I made," he reports, "is not controlling my schedule. I was not prepared for the demands on my time—internally or externally."

Years ago I penned an article on business strategy—and gained the derision of my quantitatively minded McKinsey colleagues by saying that the single most significant strategic issue facing any leader was the allocation of time. We *are* how we spend our time. Whether your name is George W. Bush. Or H. Lee Scott.

Amen.

Yes, amen. As I sat glued to my chair—I inhaled this book at one reading—that's mostly what I kept saying:

"Amen."

This book is not about rocket science. It's about people confronting enormously complex challenges . . . and keeping it simple. And human. Holding themselves to a handful of (in retrospect!) self-evident truths. By telling the truth. Obsessing on talent. Listening to the customer. Acting fast—long before "perfect information" is available. Controlling the calendar. Getting out and about and not becoming trapped by "headquartersitis."

Brilliant.

I present one hundred seminars a year. I use PowerPoint slides to punctuate my remarks. After reading this book, I created a single slide to encapsulate what these extraordinary leaders had shared with us readers. It looked like this:

> Provide a simple, clear, exciting, and energizing focus. ("Create a 'cause,' not a 'business,'" says strategy guru Gary Hamel.)

Obsess on *talent*. (Talent is a 24/7 preoccupation for many of the best bosses.)

Speed beats perfection. (Quick decision-making provides the basis for clarity, motivation, and rapid adjustment.)

"Leap" beats limp/"line extension." (Beware "me too"; i.e., perfecting yesterday—and ignoring the day after tomorrow.)

Brands that matter are sensual. (It ain't about the advertising—it is about the abiding emotional appeal, of a magazine or a Pentium processor.)

Tell the truth. (Architects of change must maintain their credibility—first and foremost.)

Control your calendar. (It's all you have. And it never lies about what really counts with the leader: 20 percent of your time on talent? Then you're not a "talent guy.")

Get out of the office. (All leaders are under constant threat of losing touch, and being captured by cronies.)

Listen to customers. (The customer knows more about you than you do. Open your ears and your heart to their heartfelt pleas—I just went through

this in one of my businesses; it was traumatic, and
invaluable.)

Oddly, the events of September 11, 2001, play into these
themes. As I've said, this book is not about rocket science.
And at a time of stress and confusion, clear messages and
images have never been more important. Leaders who stir
their followers—Welch of GE or Giuliani of NYC—strike
basic resonant chords within us. Cases in point: Gandhi.
Churchill. Roosevelt. Reagan.

Leadership, it turns out, is excruciatingly complex . . .
and excruciatingly simple. And this book makes a truly significant contribution to the often insipid literature of leadership. Moreover, it's as relevant to a twenty-six-year-old
neophyte as it is to a newly appointed CEO of Big Corp.

Part One

Motivating Your Employees

Jack Welch

CHAIRMAN AND
CHIEF EXECUTIVE
OF GENERAL
ELECTRIC CO.

As chairman and chief executive of General Electric Co. for nearly two decades, Jack Welch has reshaped the company through more than six hundred acquisitions and achieved one earnings record after another. Yet he says his most important job—the one he devotes more time to than any other— is motivating and assessing GE's employees.

"You have to go along with a can of fertilizer in one hand and water in the other and constantly throw both on the flowers," he says. "If they grow, you have a beautiful garden. If they don't, you cut them out. That's what management is all about."

WSJ: What did you learn about motivating people from your first management job?

WELCH: I had the luxury of starting as the first employee of a new plastics operation at General Electric. When I hired my first person, we were a team of two. I didn't see myself as a boss but as a peer. The two of us hired a third employee, and then more.

We had all of the things you have in a small start-up. We went to my house for dinner. We met on the weekends. We socialized. We worked Saturdays. We didn't have any pomp and circumstance, and we didn't have any memos. It was like the family grocery store, which is what we always called [our business].

I think ideally that is how a company works. It becomes a place of ideas, not a place of position.

WSJ: Is it still a grocery store?

WELCH: As any business matures, it runs into problems of hierarchy. But there is still spirit and a party atmosphere. When you win, you celebrate. We used to have the Hundred-Pound-Order Club. Whenever we got to a hundred pounds, we would ring a bell and stop [the assembly line] and everyone would go bonkers. I see elements of that today in different businesses at GE.

WSJ: Did you have a particular boss who inspired you?

WELCH: In my first sixteen years at GE, I never worked in the same town as my boss, so in some ways I never had a boss. But my first job was in Pittsfield, Mass., and I had a disaster once when a plant blew up. I had to go down to Connecticut to see my bosses and explain what had happened, and they couldn't have been more supportive and encouraging.

I clearly learned you have to make mistakes. Here I'd blown up a plant and I wasn't fired. I wasn't yelled at or even criticized.

WSJ: How did the frustrations you felt as an up-and-comer shape your management style?

WELCH: Initially, I was part of a workplace where the reward system was incredibly level. I was on a small project, like several other GE newcomers. At the end of the year, we all got the exact same thousand-dollar raise. I said, "This isn't for me, I have to get out of here." But my boss asked me to stay, and I never had that problem again.

That experience made me aware of what the frustrations can be for others in a large company like GE. You drive into the big parking lot, put your car among rows and rows of other cars, go into the office, and some horse's ass tells you what to do and how to do it. And this isn't what you expected out of life. If you don't get recognized and you have the wrong boss, it can be awful.

WSJ: What do you advise employees to do?

WELCH: I tell people to never allow themselves to become victims in an institution. Because many people end up feeling like victims. They are in the wrong job, or they have plateaued, or they don't want to rock the boat.

I encourage them to raise their hands, to be seen, to make a statement. I tell them, "If GE can't be the place where you can get rid of that victim feeling, go somewhere else." And we try to weed out the managers who make employees feel like victims, the managers who lose staff all the time.

WSJ: How much time do you spend on people issues?

WELCH: At least 50 percent of my time. I'll show you. [He pulls out a huge notebook filled with charts that rate each professional in one unit.] Here would be the vitality rating. Everyone knows where they are.

1's are the top 10 percent. These are the top people. 2's are the next-strongest 15 percent. 3's are the middle 50 percent. The ones in the middle have a real future. Then 4's are the caution 15 percent. They can move to the left. 5's are the least effective 10 percent. We've got to get rid of them. We don't want to see these people again.

On every performance appraisal they are being told you are at 1, 2, 3, 4, or 5. So no one will ever come in with any chance to say, "I was always told I was great. And now you are telling me I am not great."

WSJ: And your rating affects your chance at stock options, right?

WELCH: All the 1's will get options. About 90 percent-plus of the 2's will get options. About half of the 3's will get options. And the 4's get no stock options.

See, there's an option chart in here. Who got options? Who didn't? Here it says what happens. . . . Are they out? How did you reward these people? Do you want to love and hug these people? Kiss them? Nurture them? Give them everything?

WSJ: What is that like for them? In a sense, they are all up against each other then. Doesn't that put a lot of stress on them?

WELCH: No. There is plenty of room. See, 3's are okay. This is not punishing 3's. This is not at all that. I don't know if this is more rigorous than other companies. But I think it is our product.

WSJ: In this example, it's broken down evenly: 10 percent are 1, 15 percent are 2, 50 percent are 3, 15 percent are 4 and 10 percent are 5. Do you always grade on a curve?

WELCH: We demand it of every group. Because every group will fight like hell to say, I have all 1's. If I get ten people, one is a 1 and one is a 5.

WSJ: How do you know when to cut somebody loose?

WELCH: With the 5's it is clear as a bell. I think they know it. And you know it. It isn't even a hard conversation. It is better for everyone. They go on to a new place, a new life, a new start.

The decision is harder with the 4's. The difference between a 1 and a 3, though, is not that little a jump. It is 10 people. It is 15 people. When you get the top 10 percent performers, their output and energizing impact is overwhelming compared to 4's.

WSJ: How do you motivate those average employees?

WELCH: By telling them they can get to be 2's and 1's, and telling them they are eligible for options. But only the best of them will get options.

WSJ: How many actually get options?

WELCH: We have about 85,000 professionals. And we give options to 10,000 to 12,000 a year—but not always to the same people. So about one third of our people, about 29,000, have gotten options, although not all in any one year.

WSJ: Do you give people goals to improve their performance?

WELCH: I think goals are less helpful than knowing they are not at a dead end. We want to grow this company as fast as we can. I think that is about as specific a goal as I ought to be setting. Because I want to let them think up a zillion ways to grow. If I know what to do, what do I need them for?

Some companies have contracts with their employees. I hate those. If you and I are making a contract, and I am the boss, what are you likely to do for the week before we meet? You are going to work out fifty charts to prove to me that you can't do too much. And I am going to try to pull you higher. And in the end we will compromise. On the other hand, if I turn to you and say I want every growth idea you have in your body—and I ask, "What do you need, do you need more people, do you need more research and development?"—you will come in with all kinds of things that I have never thought about. Then I can say, "I don't like that idea, I don't want to do that one, but I would like to do that one." The dialogue between us is so much richer.

WSJ: How do you encourage risk-taking and mistakes when you also require results?

WELCH: I talked before about the disadvantage of working in a big company, the numbing feeling you can have in the parking lot. But there's also an advantage to being huge.

Last year we made 108 acquisitions for $21 billion. That's 108 swings. Every one of those acquisitions had a perfect plan. But we know 20 percent or 30 percent will blow up in our face.

A small company can only make one or two bets or they go out of business. But we can afford to make lots more mistakes, and in fact we have to throw more things at the wall. The big companies that get into trouble are those that try to manage their size instead of experimenting with it.

WSJ: How do you get your message down through the ranks?

WELCH: I would never want to run this company without Crotonville [GE's management training center in Crotonville, New York]. About five thousand people go through there each year. I will see about a thousand myself for four hours, plus another two hours at the bar.

WSJ: Aren't you also known for sending personal notes to managers?

WELCH: I just became an e-mail person. And one executive I e-mailed wrote back saying he couldn't stand my new skill. He said, "How will I know without that big black scribble across the top of the page—with the width of the scribble determining the angst with which you are writing—how you feel?"

WSJ: How involved do you get in GE's distinct businesses?

WELCH: My job is not to know everything about each business. It is to pick the people who will run the business and to decide how much money Business A versus Business B or C gets—and how to transfer people, dollars, and ideas across those businesses. I don't get into the how. So I get into trouble when I get on the golf course with someone from a particular industry who wants to know how the widget is built. I am out of gas then.

WSJ: When it comes to recognizing employees, what counts more, financial rewards or the personal touch?

WELCH: I think showering rewards on people for excellence is an important part of the management process. There's nothing I like more than giving big raises. I don't want anyone with his nose against the glass, I want them to go right through the glass—maybe because I had my nose against the glass.

You have to get rewarded in the soul and the wallet. The money isn't enough, but a plaque isn't enough either. Years ago I worked for somebody who was giving out medals to employees who got patents. I wanted to give them more cash. This guy was a fat cat who had a lot of money. He said money is so crass, just give them the medal. I just thought that was wrong; you have to give both.

WSJ: How do you evaluate your top executives? Do you rate them against each other?

WELCH: I compare them against their competition, and never against each other. We have one plan where half the reward an executive gets is for the performance of his business and half for the performance of the whole company. But if the company doesn't make it and the business has a greater performance, the bonus is zero—because no boats get to the shore if the *Titanic* sinks.

WSJ: How important is it to feel attuned with the people you manage?

WELCH: It doesn't matter if you don't want to hang around with them or socialize with them. It doesn't matter if someone doesn't like baseball or libraries or museums or opera or they dress differently than you. But if your business values are different, if your treatment of people is different, if you don't agree about the behavior you want to cultivate in your company, that is a problem. You have to be on the same page there.

wsj: How do you overcome employees' intimidation when in your presence?

WELCH: This is a hard question, because I don't really know if they feel intimidated. But we have a lot of humor in our company. We spend a lot of time screwing around.

Our meetings are not always the most productive. Like, for example, the other Monday: We spent the first half hour talking about Saturday's golf tournament, and everybody was screaming about the putts. And we had the most crazy, packed day.

wsj: You've been identified with GE for so long. How will your successor establish his own identity?

WELCH: By being himself and doing it his way. It will take some time. It takes everyone time. But we are so deep. We

---

Five Lessons from Jack Welch on Motivation

1. Tell people to never allow themselves to become victims. . . . They should go somewhere else if that's how they feel.

2. Constantly refine your gene pool . . . by promoting your best performers and weeding out your worst.

3. Grade on a curve. . . . If I get ten people, one is a star and one won't cut it.

4. Instead of giving people specific operating goals, challenge them to give you every growth idea they've got.

5. You can't just reward people with trophies. Reward them in the wallet, too.

have so many people. This is so much less of a one-man show than the world will ever give it credit for being. They are all sitting there saying, "I would like to do this this way. I would like to do that that way. And why is that jerk doing that?" That is the way life is.

Steve Ballmer

CHIEF EXECUTIVE
OF MICROSOFT
CORPORATION

When he took over as chief executive of Microsoft Corp. in January 2000, Steve Ballmer assumed day-to-day responsibility for one of the most influential companies driving the American economy—and one that, until recently, had the largest stock-market value of any U.S. business.

But things change quickly in the go-go world of technology. Microsoft's power is in danger of being eclipsed by new Internet technologies as well as by networked computer systems that run off centralized "server" machines instead of loaded-up personal computers powered by Microsoft's ubiquitous Windows operating system.

A more immediate threat at the time of this interview in June 2000: the controversial order by a federal judge to break

Microsoft into two separate companies. The judge also wanted to impose harsh business restrictions to curb what he calls Microsoft's monopoly power. (In June 2001, a federal appeals court voided Judge Thomas Penfield Jackson's order for Microsoft's breakup, but found that Microsoft had abused its power.)

In an interview by phone from London, where he was in the midst of a trip visiting customers in seven European countries, the always enthusiastic Mr. Ballmer explained how he would manage it all.

WSJ: This is an extraordinary time for the company, with Microsoft facing complex legal issues and serious competitive threats. How has your management style changed to deal with these pressures?

BALLMER: We have a supercharged element in our company's history. . . . When you have that kind of supercharged element, at times it reminds you of what's key to really focus on. There are three things broadly to focus on. Number one, you've got to make sure you've got great people . . . you have to rededicate yourself to those key people. . . . Number two, you have to refocus in on clear, simple goals . . . it helps people have a weather vane, so maybe when things aren't so supercharged, you could live without [as much direction].

Number three . . . you've got to have a clear, thought-leading proposition for people to say, "I know what we're doing today, I know what our goals are today, I know how that fits into the bigger picture." . . . You need to engage people in where it is you're going in a serious way and have

them really feel it and be enthused by it. . . . They need a
mission.

WSJ: How can you press forward with major new strategy ini-
tiatives, like your new next-generation Internet-software
push, when being aggressive and dominating a new market may be held against you in court?

BALLMER: You can't be ambiguous about what you think the
law lets you do. . . . The law, the order given by the appel-
late court, clearly says that as long as there's plausible benefit, you're allowed to enhance and improve your products.
You can't believe in that and then not act on it. I don't
know what benefit it brings you to not act on it.

If the ruling as issued was ever to actually be enforced, it
would be so bad for consumers around the world . . . so bad
in terms of reduced innovation. Not by smaller companies.
But they'll be reducing the innovation coming out of the
biggest R&D spender in the software business, Microsoft.
They will reduce innovation. And raise prices.

You have no choice but to press forward. . . . This judge
does seem to disagree, and that's his prerogative.

WSJ: You previously mentioned employee retention. Just how
do you keep employees motivated through all this?

BALLMER: Well, you've got to make sure that you really ask, do
we have for everyone jobs that are big enough for them—
but not too big? Does everyone see clearly what their
mission is? Are you spending enough time with people one-
on-one? Are you hearing what they have to say about
what they need? Are you making sure that you don't keep
people around who are not contributing? When they've
been around a long time, that's kind of hard. I'm a guy

who's a very loyal guy . . . I don't want to see them go. They're friends. They're family. Sometimes you have to understand that it's the right thing [for them to leave] . . . it's better for them and it's better for the company.

WSJ: But what specifically have you been doing over the last few months in terms of employee morale and retention?

BALLMER: I think we have all asked ourselves to make sure we're really engaging with our teams. I'm spending more time with my staff and our so-called business-leadership team, which is kind of our senior-vice-president-on-up group. . . . I'm pushing to really engage and stay close and involved with their staff. We're also doing more one-to-many outreach. About an hour ago, I finished, with Bill and our senior people, a presentation via Windows media technologies to about 35,000 employees so that they could understand our view of what happened and didn't happen.

WSJ: What did you tell them?

BALLMER: We told them things are going to be fine. The future's so bright, we gotta wear shades. Here's why we have integrity. . . . And we tried to say that in a very open, direct way.

WSJ: Are you hearing from employees, perhaps through e-mails, that they're disheartened and are wondering why they should stay at Microsoft?

BALLMER: I'm not hearing from employees. It's not the world I live in. The world I live in, the [Department of Justice] case, I mean, when you get out of Redmond, it gets even more absurd. People are just focused in on what they have to do. . . . Leave because of the DOJ case? It doesn't come up much. The people who leave, leave us because they're overwhelmed . . . or they leave because they see an exciting new opportunity. Although I've got to say, people, their eyes are a little less glazy now that the Nasdaq has come down.

Or they leave because we didn't have them in the right job. They leave because we didn't have them in a job that was exciting. That's our fault. Nobody's told me ever that they've left because of the DOJ case.

WSJ: For a couple of years now, even prelawsuit, some have said Microsoft has grown too big, too bureaucratic, too political—and that's why some high-level executives have left for start-ups. Is this a problem? And what do you do to keep decision-making streamlined?

BALLMER: I think having a clear framework for where the opportunity is, in the future, is key. You give people within that framework a lot of flexibility to do that job. And when the framework isn't clear, things become tougher.

WSJ: So have you done anything to take decision-making layers out of the process?

BALLMER: We haven't taken layers out. You need a clear framework. I certainly know [that] when you don't have a clear framework, a clear, thought-leading vision, that's not a good thing for a variety of reasons. That's why I'm so excited to put in place the framework [of Next Generation Windows Services, the firm's new Web software initiative].

WSJ: You spoke earlier about the need during these times to have clear, simple goals. What are your goals right now?

BALLMER: We have short-term and long-term. Short-term, I think we clearly have to drive success at the desktop level around Windows 2000 and Office. But with Windows 2000, I don't think we've done a great job always of telling this story about how great Windows 2000 is on the desktop even if you're not implementing Windows 2000 on the server. . . .

The development teams and the sales teams have to keep riveted on that.

Number two short-term goal: We have an incredible story, an incredible product, an incredible lineup to help people with their mission-critical, enterprise e-commerce applications. Windows 2000, the data-center server, the work we're doing in SQL Server, applications centered on the next generation . . . we have a clear opportunity to change the way people feel about creating applications.

Number three: MSN [Microsoft's Internet-access service and collection of websites]. We've got a lot of momentum these days with MSN. . . . In a number of the last few months we've been ahead of Yahoo! in both reach and usage. . . . We're coming up strongly in a variety of different places.

Last is kind of the bridge between long-term and short-term—the NGWS vision . . . the work we're doing in mobility and wireless. The work we're doing in TV. The work we're doing in small-business services.

Number four is NGWS and those things that dovetail.

WSJ: But how do you enunciate these goals? Are they posted up in hallways on Microsoft's campus, the way companies like Merrill Lynch post lists of their core values?

BALLMER: The principles which we talk about, our values, those are things that never change. Goals, I'd say, are things that do change.

Our values—integrity, innovation, partnership, customer focus—those things don't change. But . . . I've got lots of slides that have these points on them. I stick them up every place I talk.

WSJ: How do you keep yourself motivated and enthusiastic in these difficult times?

BALLMER: I think I'm a pretty positive person . . . I like to be up. And if you get too down, get on the road. Get out there. See customers and understand how much of a positive impact you're having. Understand how much of this you have to do. For me it's energizing.

Sometimes I get tired. I don't sleep that well because our guys usually work me till twelve at night. I get up at five-thirty to go jogging. We're moving, we're working, we're seeing people. It's energizing to see these partners. They want to know, What about this? What about that? I was in Holland today, where we had about two thousand people to talk to about e-commerce and the future of the Internet. This morning we talked to CEOs. You can just see that opportunity so clearly.

WSJ: Judge Thomas Penfield Jackson had some very harsh words for Microsoft and its executives, saying you've failed to admit that you've done anything wrong, and that the company has been "untrustworthy" in the past. What's your reaction to that? How do you explain that to employees?

BALLMER: I certainly know that we win the trust of our customers and our employees every day. They know us.

They've been with us through this ride. I've been with Bill Gates for twenty-five years. I know I'm a person of integrity. I feel good about myself.

The fact of the matter is, we still believe, as I think the law tells us to believe, that we have an ability and a right and even an obligation under the law to improve our products. I think Judge Jackson didn't believe that. He didn't believe that at the time of the consent decree. We may disagree about that. I know we're honest, forthright people, and our customers know that and our employees know that.

WSJ: Even though you disagree with Judge Jackson's ruling and plan to appeal, do you have contingency plans in the works in case the appeal fails? Have you thought about whether you'd join the operating system or the applications company?

BALLMER: We're working hard on our appeal. We're working hard on our business. That's what we're working on. We're working hard on our request for a stay [of the judge's most immediate business-conduct remedies].

I think the consequences to the consumer [of the judge's order] are so strongly bad that we need to put our efforts into those areas.

Part Two

Managing
Growth

John Chambers

When John Chambers was named chief executive of Cisco Systems, Inc., in January 1995, the computer-networking equipment maker had three thousand employees and sales of approximately $2 billion a year. Today, Cisco is a telecommunications behemoth, with thirty thousand employees and annual revenues nearing $20 billion. Cisco has grown into the third-most-valuable company in the world, at one point reaching a market capitalization of $541 billion.

As it diversifies into fiber-optic communications gear and other new fields, Cisco continues to grow at an astonishing rate, exceeding 50 percent a year. It adds a thousand employees a month and devours, on average, a high-tech start-up every two weeks.

Since late March 2000, amid concerns about its lofty valuation and investors' retreat from tech stocks, Cisco's high-flying stock price has lost some of its altitude, declining by more than one fourth and erasing more than $100 billion in market capitalization. Although the share price remains more than double the level of 1999 and roughly on pace with the company's ten-year trajectory, the recent decline raises questions about Cisco's ability to keep its employees and potential acquisition targets happy.

How do you run a company growing that fast, with a stock that volatile? In interviews in May 2000, Mr. Chambers offered some tips.

WSJ: How has the recent decline in Cisco's stock affected your ability to recruit employees and complete acquisitions?

CHAMBERS: The market's ups and downs in large part don't affect our decision-making here at Cisco. . . . We've always made decisions based on what we think is best for our employees and shareholders and the company in the long run, and not on the short-run gyrations in the stock market.

We've been very open with employees in particular, that we want them to view the opportunity for the long run. That's why we extended [the vesting period of our] options from four years to five years and why we pass out options every year. It's why we wouldn't reprice options.

While it may sound callous, it's easier for us to operate in a tough market than it is in an up market. [Our stock doesn't fluctuate as much as others'.] So companies that weren't interested in being acquired as recently as a month ago are now interested in being acquired. . . . The last couple of months [the gyrating market] hasn't had any impact other than making it easier to acquire. It's the same thing with employees. There are a lot of employees at start-ups who have seen their net worth erode very quickly or their options [go] underwater, so it makes it easier for us to recruit them.

WSJ: At a time when Microsoft is on the verge of being broken up, how has Cisco avoided antitrust scrutiny?

CHAMBERS: I'd be shocked and extremely disappointed if this were to be an issue for Cisco. . . . [We operate on] open standards and [there is a] lack of barriers of entry into the marketplace. . . . Four hundred to five hundred start-ups have entered the market against us in the last eighteen months. Then there's our position in the market. For data, voice, and video combined, we have less than a 10 percent market share. There is only going to be one network in the future [combining these elements], and we still have a relatively small piece. . . .

I learned the hard way at IBM and Wang [Laboratories] that competition is good for you. Competition is what forces you to move faster. . . . You don't view competitors as the bad guy. They are actually the good guys in terms of what they are doing to customer life that forces us to act quicker. We will have more market share three to five years from now because we have good competitors.

We have a culture that accepts competition in a very positive way, that doesn't try to stifle or kill competition.

[My rule is], you never do something to someone else that you would have a problem with if they did [it] to you.

WSJ: How do you manage differently today than when you took over?

CHAMBERS: Part of the answer may surprise you. A lot of the basics haven't changed. The approach that we started in '93 was one of segmenting the market, being number one and number two in each segment and each product area . . . , and [devising] our strategy to make that happen. . . . [We were] very much focused on how we used systems to gain competitive advantage and allow the scaling of the company to cookie-cut ideas. . . . We're now to the point where we actually can scale pretty rapidly. . . . It might surprise you, but there isn't a lot of difference . . . if you manage—let me use the term "lead" as opposed to "manage"—if you lead that way, whether you're two thousand people, twenty thousand, or a hundred thousand people.

WSJ: How do you "cookie-cut" ideas?

CHAMBERS: We don't do something that, if it works well, we wouldn't replicate. So we try to set it up in a way that, if it's really successful, it's replicable across the whole company. Without that attention to discipline, you can't scale with the speed that is needed. . . .

WSJ: Are there things a CEO can't do in a company this large?

CHAMBERS: My goal hasn't changed in terms of having responsibility for setting the strategy at Cisco . . . that's one of the top three things I do. The second thing that I do is recruit and develop and retain the leadership team that is going to be able to implement that strategy.

The third thing that I do is really focus on what culture we want here at Cisco. . . . And it hasn't changed. The leader must walk his or her talk. So if you say customer success is most important, I still listen to every critical account in the world every night. Now, we have a process that works like clockwork behind that, but it's one of the areas I haven't changed.

WSJ: How does it work?

CHAMBERS: When a network is unstable, that's a critical A. When a network has the potential of becoming unstable and we've got to watch it, that's a B. So I get a report on all critical A accounts in the world. Now, the fact that we focus on it so heavily helps us to resolve it quicker but also helps us to prevent it. So I get a report each evening on anywhere from zero to fifteen [accounts]. If there are only a few, then probably we haven't made enough new boxes out there. If it begins to get up to double digits, then we've got a customer-satisfaction issue coming our way. . . .

Then we pay every manager on customer satisfaction. It's amazing how that works. Once you say it's going to be part of their compensation, people say, "This must really be important," and second, "John's going to ask me about it all the time." And for either reason, they respond very well.

In our most recent survey, [customer-satisfaction scores] went up tremendously around the world. [There is a] one-to-one correlation between customer satisfaction and future revenues and profits.

The problem is that it lags twelve to twenty-four months, which is why most American companies don't pay as much attention to it as I believe that they should. Case in point: When I saw Dell's customer satisfaction go up dramatically . . . I knew that they would be a good stock five years ago.

WSJ: You mentioned recruiting top talent. What do you look for in your managers?

CHAMBERS: People talk about vision or instinct. . . . Your ability to lead is based upon your life's experience. Part of it is education. Part of that is the values you grew up with. . . . The largest part is the experience you've had in multiple stages of leadership over your career. . . .

I believe you've got to articulate to your team what you expect of them and what you're going to hold them accountable for. So at the heart of that is getting the results. . . . The [second] key element of a leader is, how good is your team? If you ask, "What's going to get the result?" it actually is the quality of the team that is the key determining factor—the ability to attract, retain, and develop—and you've got to develop at the speed that we're growing.

The mathematics of this are interesting. If you grow at 50 percent per [year] for eighteen months . . . it requires you to double your leadership team every eighteen months, just mathematically to stay where you were before.

The third element is trust and integrity. . . . The fourth element is industry knowledge. . . . The fifth element is teamwork, and I'm a nut on teamwork. . . .

The sixth element is communication skills . . . and this is becoming more and more a requirement, particularly for leadership higher in the organization. . . . It isn't [just] one-on-one communications anymore; it's, how do you get your message across? My average presentation today, probably half of them are in front of five hundred people or more. . . . And a large part of communication skills, which people forget, is [listening]. . . . Your ability to listen as the company gets bigger also becomes more of a challenge, because you can't walk around and touch like you used to. You've got to learn how to do that in groups. . . .

[The seventh is] customer focus. . . . You've got to say, does each one of our leaders, regardless of what function they're in, really think, "Customer first"? It's amazing when you go to other companies and you sit in on their meetings, how sometimes the word "customer" never comes up. It's actually scary. . . . [Eighth is] balancing planning and reacting. . . . We are probably world-class at reacting, and when you're really good at the diving catches, if you're not careful you can dive and catch too often. . . . The next element is people skills. . . . And then, finally, can you drive Cisco's culture?

WSJ: With thirty thousand employees, how do you stay in touch with the front lines?

CHAMBERS: Well, if you add time together with the customers and with our own employees, that's probably 70 percent of my time. And sometimes they overlap. When you call on your customers, you're often with your local team. . . . I rank [each VP and senior VP] each quarter, top to bottom, about how many [customer] visits did they participate in and what their evaluation [was] from the customers.

WSJ: Do you still meet with groups of frontline employees
every month?

CHAMBERS: The birthday breakfasts are probably the most
valuable sessions I do with employees. Once a month, anybody who has a birthday in that month can come and quiz
[me] for about an hour and a half, and anything is fair
game. We deliberately asked directors and VPs not to participate, so that people who I don't get a chance normally
to listen to can participate. And every single time, I learn
two or three things that either I need to do differently, or
things that I thought were working one way weren't.

But again, it's building the culture. You want to lead by
example. If you do that as a CEO, that will filter down
through the leadership style of your team, where they'll do
meetings with their employees and listen to their team.

WSJ: How do you keep track of Cisco's diverse products and
customers?

CHAMBERS: This is where the Web-based architecture is so
key, because I can see an automatic roll-up [summary] of
customer satisfaction very quickly any time I want. I can
see an automatic roll-up of every order around the world
and explode that down, not just by key geographies, and I
look at every geography every day. So I look at my four key
theaters, then I can explode it down to if I want to see by
country or by city or by key customer, even down to an
individual sales rep. . . . And then we, I, listen to construc-
tive criticism probably more—not probably, definitely a lot
more—than you do compliments. Compliments are nice,
and I always need them, but I really listen to what we need
to do better very, very carefully.

[The key is], how do you put a lot of the day-to-day activities down one layer, and then over time down two, and then over time down three? And now the decisions that [once] would have come to the CEO might be made by the first-line manager.

So for example . . . margins. Very often at the end of a quarter I might have realized that we had a problem in one of our product lines, that we didn't meet our margin expectations on it. Well, today the first-line manager can see who has responsibility for that product, either in engineering or in manufacturing, [and] that the second week into the quarter our margins aren't in line with what we expected. They can explode that information down because of our use of Web-based architecture to understand exactly [what happened]: Are we discounting too heavily again? Is it because we're seeing more competition on a global basis, therefore we had to adjust, pricewise? . . . You can explode out your orders that are in the process so you can see: Will it correct itself or is it something that's going to get worse?

Well, those decisions used to come to the CFO and CEO two to three weeks after every quarter was closed. That now is done by the first-line manager any time they want to look into it. That's what empowerment is all about. That's what the Internet is about. It's about empowerment.

WSJ: You run this company without a defined number two. Why?

CHAMBERS: I think if you signal who's going to be your replacement too early, you put that person into a no-win situation. [And] you put other people into career decisions that may not be in the best interest of the company. So my

own view is that probably within the last year before I
leave I will signal, very vividly and very directly, who my
replacement will be—and that assumes that I don't mess
up along the way and the board [replaces] me, or my
employees lose confidence or shareholders lose confidence
in me. . . .

I think companies like GE have shown how important
[waiting to designate a successor] is, in terms of both keeping the talent together but also giving people a chance.
Because the person who's most likely to be that person
today may very well not be [that person] three or four
years from now.

I will over time, however, have to empower a COO type
of position in the company or one to two key leaders that
I'll load more onto. You've got to have that responsibility
in order to scale. So at some time in the future you will see
me probably move with a COO just to pull part of the load.
That's not an indication they are my successor, but it does
mean that I've got to have one or two people who I give
more responsibility to for the company.

WSJ: That's very different from your own experience. You
came in, several years before you became CEO, as a clear
number two, and with a promise of being number one.
Wasn't that a good idea, or was that just a different time?

CHAMBERS: Well, it was different time, different place, different age and leader. [Chairman and former chief executive]
John Morgridge made a decision for personal reasons that
he didn't want to stay as the CEO and president of the
company and he would want to move on to chairman, and
that he wanted a different skill set, somebody who was

going to be in it for, potentially if things went well, the next ten-plus years. . . . And we didn't miss a beat.

By the time I was announced as CEO, I already had everybody reporting to me, and John went off and rode a bike in Vietnam for four months. So the transition had been one of the smoothest ever. But it was very clear that John didn't want to stay in the leadership role and that he needed to be able to answer that question to the shareholders, to the board, and to our employees.

WSJ: As fast as you've grown, you've got ambitious plans to grow even more, including the campus you're planning for

---

Five Lessons from John Chambers on Managing Growth

1. Make your customers the center of your culture. Cisco ties employee compensation programs directly to customer-satisfaction results.
2. Empower every employee: You will increase productivity and improve retention.
3. Thrive on change.
4. Teamwork requires open, two-way communication and trust.
5. Build strong partnerships. Leading companies this decade will focus on internal development, effective acquisitions, and also forming an ecosystem of partnerships in a horizontal business model.

another twenty thousand people. Isn't there a little bit of hubris in planning for that many more people?

CHAMBERS: Today, we still do most of our [planning] in the two-year scenario, but for product development we can go out to three-plus years, and, oddly enough, the area that we plan most for is campuses. To get a campus selected, to acquire it, to work it through the appropriate government and other entities that have an influence over that, and to get your building started and up almost requires three to five years now.

If we're fortunate enough to become a $50 billion company in the next four to five years, and that depends on how well we execute—but the market will support it, with or without Cisco, if it isn't us it will be somebody else—we would need probably 100,000 employees.

Having said that, I also have the healthy paranoia. Every single building here and in [the new campus] will be built all with a separate entrance, a separate utility pattern. So if we ever had to, we could sell each one individually or lease each one individually. I learned that the hard way at Wang Laboratories.

Juergen Schrempp

CHAIRMAN AND CEO
OF DAIMLER-
CHRYSLER AG

Juergen Schrempp calls them "digital" decisions: uncompromising yes/no determinations that a computer might make. "We promised ourselves, let's put the unpopular issues on the table right from the start," says the chairman and CEO of DaimlerChrysler AG.

As it happened, his lengthy 1999 interview with The Wall Street Journal *came on the eve of a revolution that is rocking one of the great experiments under way in global business: the merger of automotive giants Daimler-Benz AG with Chrysler Corp.*

Mr. Schrempp frankly acknowledged that change was coming and characterized it as consistent with his determination to manage the merger by making tough, fast calls, even if they prove unpopular.

WSJ: Was there a critical lesson you learned at the outset of the merger?

SCHREMPP: I coined the phrase . . . "the danger of [a] deadly wish for harmony." . . . You put two companies together, you have two general counsels, two internal auditors, you have two communications chiefs, etc., etc., etc. What guys who had problems did was say, "Well, we come together, we are all one family, we love each other, we kiss each other." And we promised ourselves—not that we were entirely successful in doing it—but we promised ourselves, "Let's put the unpopular issues on the table right from the start." . . . By the way, people, human beings, don't like digital decisions, they like compromises. . . .

WSJ: What kind of decisions are digital?

SCHREMPP: A digital decision is a yes or no. A digital decision is, you have two general counsels, one will be the boss. [Some people in mergers that had trouble would say,] "No, no, no, let's make an arrangement, let's say, well, we have two general counsels [and] run it together." [But] we said no.

We went through the list, and for example . . . the general counsel in a U.S. company is so much more important than in Germany. . . . As a chief executive of a German company, I can make decisions without consulting a lawyer. I don't think many do it in America. . . .

So my guy [the Daimler general counsel] came to me and said, "Look, I have to admit, the [American general counsel] is good, and I have to admit, we're operating in the U.S. But I've been number one, and I would stay number one. And seeing as I can't do it here, let's make a deal.

And we did a deal, and [the German counsel] left. This was not picked up by the American media, because it's not important there.

Then we needed a communications head [and] we decided Christoph Walther would be the guy. . . . [The] U.S. guy, a very good guy, decided . . . , "Why should I actually report to Christoph Walther—I was the chief. So, I'm moving. . . ."

WSJ: Why did you feel you had to make yes-or-no people decisions?

SCHREMPP: For psychological reasons. . . . If you come together, and you say . . . "Let's just [mark time] for the next twelve, eighteen months, we're not changing anything. . . . Let [people] be comfortable." Totally wrong! You know, they actually expect changes. However, if you don't change anything substantially in the first twelve, eighteen months, they get into what I call a static position. . . . The resistance to change once they feel comfortable again is so much greater than if you change during the time that they expect changes anyway. . . .

The other [issue] that was really important was speed. Now, speed could mean, occasionally, that you make mistakes. My principle always was . . . move as fast as you can and [if] you indeed make mistakes, you have to correct them. . . . It's much better to move fast and make mistakes occasionally than to move too slowly.

WSJ: Can you give us an example of a mistake that needed correcting?

SCHREMPP: Well, you have written about them. . . . We wanted a merger of equals very much in spirit. . . . And obviously we wanted to have pooling of interests, don't forget that. . . . And that's why we started this company off with eighteen board members. . . .

[Then] we . . . had our first top management meeting, just after the closing. . . . And the people asked us, the senior people asked us, "Do you really want to run this company with eighteen people?" And we said, "For now, yes." We were honest. We said, "Look, we have to refine that further, in something of an evolutionary process. That will be our next step. And the next step is imminent."

WSJ: There's a lot of anxiety in a deal like this. How do you manage the anxiety part?

SCHREMPP: I was in . . . a town hall meeting [near the Auburn Hills, Michigan, headquarters of Chrysler]. This time it was in a tent because they [were opening a Chrysler] museum. . . . There were 350 people there. . . . I had a speech of, I don't know, thirty pages, and I looked at these people, and I said, the last thing they wanted is for me to recite this speech. So I asked a few people to come together beforehand, and I said, "Now give me all the perceptions, the facts, the nonsense going on here. . . . Whether fact or not, I'm not interested. Perception is as important as fact." . . .

I talked a little about the history of the museum, and then I went through the list. . . . We had a lively discussion. . . . We didn't do it on the basis, for the first time, where they had to get up and show their face and tell this German chairman what they don't like. They were able to write it on a card, and we went through all the cards submitted. Normally you only select the easy questions. We went through all the cards until we finished them. I think we had a discussion of an hour or so.

So there were complaints, and then I said, "Okay, fine, here you say that, I think you're right. That is what we do." Then they came to management changes, and [co-chairman Robert Eaton] earlier said to me, "Juergen, you know, we should be careful about that." And I said, "Bob, I should just be honest, because you know what feeds people—honesty." Really, I mean nobody expects honesty in this life. And I said, "Yes, I confirm, yes, we will change, yes, one or two members, or whatever, will have to leave the board. This is the background why we're doing it. And we will announce it later. . . ." Quiet. And then applause.

WSJ: Do you think that you're intimidating to people?

SCHREMPP: Well, what would you say?

WSJ: Well, I don't work for you.

SCHREMPP: I guess if I'm honest, that could occasionally be the case. I don't know what's generally the case. I tell you, if people only have access to me, let's say, once or twice a year, depending on the situation—when the stock goes down, for example—and I tell them we have to do something about it, I could possibly be intimidating. But people who are around me a lot will definitely say, "No way, he is not." But, I mean, the occasional appearances, I guess, yes.

WSJ: Is that good?

SCHREMPP: I think it's good.

WSJ: To have the fear factor?

SCHREMPP: A fear factor it's not, but hopefully, as I come to interpret it, it's . . . some respect. . . . It's not so much fear as my sometimes-too-loud voice, or whatever. I think it's the record of me being able to make very quick, unpopular decisions. Even on the German side. . . . My nickname was . . . Rambo.

WSJ: Now that you have these two cultures melding together, what's the oddest thing you've noticed about the Americans?

SCHREMPP: It's that at lunch they drink iced tea and ice water. . . . Since the merger, we had these meetings in Auburn Hills, obviously they offer me ice water and iced tea, and I'm not taking it. When we are in Stuttgart, and we have lunch, oh, they loved drinking wine. So it's not that they hate it, it's just a matter of habit.

WSJ: What have you learned about working with Americans?

SCHREMPP: What I found out . . . is that Americans are not Americans. [It] should be obvious, because . . . you have a hell of a difference between northern Germans and southern Germans. But, you know . . . I was very much exposed in my business life to Americans from the New York area. And there is . . . a difference between New York and Detroit. . . . There are many [Chrysler employees who] have lived all their lives in Detroit. Many have studied in Detroit. So they're really fixed to this area. . . . They have traveled in the United States, but they haven't so much internationally. You should not forget that Chrysler's sales were predominantly in North America—90 percent, 95 percent. Their international operations—one man [was responsible for] it, and he traveled a lot. But the others hardly traveled outside the United States, except for when there was a motor show.

So all of a sudden, this [is] something [they have] to do [and] not everybody liked it, [particularly in the beginning]. I had to take that into account. . . . I suggested, "Let's do something which is to the benefit of both. Let's have all the [management board] meetings . . . in New York." Which means . . . the German guys . . . go to London [to catch the Concorde]—three hours, twenty [minutes] to New York. It means for the Auburn Hills guys, one hour, twenty [minutes]. . . . When I suggested this in Auburn Hills they said, "This is a brilliant idea." And since that time, everybody's happy.

WSJ: Do you see the Americans becoming more German and Germans becoming more American?

SCHREMPP: I want this multicultural [element]. I want an American to stay an American. A German should stay a German. And don't forget, [we also have] Australians, South Africans, Mexicans, Brazilians. If we get them together, [then] you get the best answers. And there are yellow-skinned, black-skinned, white-skinned, different languages all around, and they argue. If that, ultimately, is the spirit of DaimlerChrysler, then we have made it. . . .

WSJ: What about the details? The Americans don't allow smoking. How do you deal with that?

SCHREMPP: These guys always go outside, and there are ashtrays outside of the building, and there they stand. . . . And I accept that we do not smoke during the meetings. . . .

WSJ: What about the Americans who come over to work in Stuttgart? Do they have a problem working in an office filled with smokers?

SCHREMPP: No, I have . . . seen quite a number of Americans smoking there. Bob [Eaton] smokes cigars . . . He has a beautiful office there in Stuttgart, and he loves to go in there and light up a cigar.

WSJ: What do employees call you? Does anybody call you by your first name?

SCHREMPP: I think in America, almost everybody does. And in Germany, [it] is starting. . . . [For Americans, pronouncing] "Schrempp" is a problem, that's why the first name is better.

Five Lessons from Juergen Schrempp on Managing a Global Megamerger

1. [Avoid] the danger of a deadly wish for harmony.
2. Put the unpopular issues on the table right from the start.
3. It's much better to move fast and make mistakes occasionally than to move too slowly.
4. The resistance to change once [employees] feel comfortable again is much greater than if you change during the time they expect changes anyway.
5. Just be honest, because you know what feeds people? Honesty. Really, I mean nobody expects honesty in this life.

WSJ: How do they say "Schrempp"?

SCHREMPP: They say it "Shrimp," and then it was only a little step to "Shrimps."

WSJ: What about meetings? Germans love to have meetings that go on and on, and Americans like to get right to the point, make a decision, and move on.

SCHREMPP:. I guess on the paper side, the cliché is a little bit right. Because . . . what the Germans generally do [is to] prepare more paper. But we have now decided [that every proposal to the board has to have] a two-page executive summary. . . . Most people . . . don't care about . . . the next twenty pages, they read that two-page executive summary.

There are lots of clichés . . . about the German side. . . . [But] I've seen Americans working. . . . It's not that different.

Sanford I. Weill

CHAIRMAN AND
CO–CHIEF EXECUTIVE
OF CITIGROUP INC.

"My whole life, I've been in a merger mode as well as a managing mode," says Sanford I. Weill. Indeed, the Wall Street executive's career is one long string of mergers. He cofounded investment bank Carter, Berlind & Weill in 1960; it became Shearson Lehman Brothers, which American Express bought in 1981. After leaving American Express, where he was president, he bought Commercial Credit Co. in 1986, later buying Primerica Corp., Travelers Group, and Salomon Bros. The deals culminated (for now) in the 1998 merger of Travelers Group and Citibank, creating Citigroup Inc.

Mr. Weill, Citigroup's chairman and co–chief executive, sat down in his New York office in the summer of 1999 for two conversations about what he has learned after a lifetime of deal-making.

WSJ: What advice would you give to all CEOs in every deal?

WEILL: Assuming that the person did all his homework, and the financials, the strategy, and the concept made sense, I would tell him to treat the other company and the people in the other company with respect. Lots of times acquisitions are of companies that are doing poorer than you are doing. And it usually is not the fault of all the people in the organization. Usually it is the fault of the leadership. You shouldn't punish everyone for that. . . .

I would tell the person he or she should make decisions faster rather than slower. . . . When you slow down that decision-making process, such as who's going to do what, the good people usually end up leaving, and you end up with a lot of mediocre performers. If you don't do things and are fiddling around, people begin to wonder, "What kind of momentum are we going to have on this ship?" . . .

And pray to God that you can keep the thing quiet so that you are not hounded by the press and forced to say something premature. Because deals really are not best done in a newspaper.

WSJ: Why do half of all mergers fail?

WEILL: Mergers fail because the people who do them are not really on top of the details of putting them together. It's like putting an engine on a car. If you don't connect it right, the car is not going to move. Doing mergers requires a company to be precision-oriented: to be faster rather than slower, to let people know where they stand.

WSJ: How do you handle the day-to-day anxiety that mergers foster among employees, especially during layoffs?

WEILL: We try to deal with that by speaking to people, by being available, by answering questions. . . . If people in a company believe that what you are doing is going to create a company that is going to end up being efficient and be able to grow again, I think they are much more willing to understand what's happening. . . . We have lots of meetings in which we include spouses. . . . We set up a thing called the spouses' breakfast, where my wife and I will have a breakfast with all the spouses and just talk about the personal side of things. . . . This is a very difficult business that requires a lot of travel, a lot of time, and a lot of anxiety, so the more a spouse knows about the people who are making their spouse anxious or come home at night not too happy, the better. You end up getting much more support from the whole household.

WSJ: The Citigroup deal came together fast . . . with some major decisions still to be made. Should you have settled more matters before announcing the deal?

WEILL: I think we discussed just about every issue that would possibly come up over the next couple of years. We didn't necessarily agree on everything. But we knew what the landscape was. We felt that it was important to get the thing done. . . . We made incredible decisions on how the stock would be split among the shareholders, what the board makeup would be, who would be on the various committees, who would be the chairman of the various committees, how the board would be compensated, thoughts on how people in the companies would be compensated. . . . You can't make all of them in advance. And if you did

make all of them in advance, you would be changing 30
percent or 40 percent of them anyway.

WSJ: Did any senior managers ask why they were kept out of
the loop?

WEILL: I had managers do that. Even my mother-in-law said,
"Why couldn't you tell me?"

WSJ: What did you tell them?

WEILL: I said, "Look, we have been partners for a long, long
time. You know as well as I do that I can't talk about these
things. You also know that we wouldn't be doing anything
unless we thought it would be in your best interest. . . . We
want to do a better job for customers, and we want to create value for our shareholders. And you are a shareholder."

WSJ: Can you give us an example of an issue where the two
companies started far apart and came together only grad-
ually?

WEILL: We talked for months about how to change benefits.
We wanted to become more modern and move away from
a defined-benefit plan to a defined-contribution plan, like
a 401(k). Citicorp had a more traditional plan for long-
term employees. Travelers [Insurance] had a decent
amount of pay based on performance. Citicorp had a lot of
[stock] options, but they didn't go very deep in the organization. Very fast, we came up with the concept of having
what we called Citigroup founders' stock options for every
employee. We wanted to do it right at the beginning so we
could get the people in the company to be on the same
page. Eventually, we ended up with a program that combined the best of both.

WSJ: Why did some businesses, like your consumer banking and insurance, come together faster than others, such as corporate banking?

WEILL: In some areas we were more successful than others, because there was less overlap of what people did, or less nervousness about how what one did might affect the relationship with another one. . . . The consumer side was somewhat easier to put together than the corporate side, where both sides were trading and both sides were in foreign exchange and both sides had been trying to build relationships with corporations. . . .

Also, on the corporate side, the Salomon and Smith Barney merger hadn't been completed yet, so that made it a little bit more difficult. Computer systems had to be worked out. We were moving people together. Some of that is just being completed.

WSJ: What brought the two companies' management teams closer together?

WEILL: At the beginning, it was creating a budget for 1999 and laying out what we hoped to accomplish over the next two or three years. . . . As results happened, we decided that we can't forever have two people doing everything and we have to begin to make some decisions and give people the authority to execute them.

WSJ: When two people are competing for one job, how do you and your co–chief executive, John Reed, determine the winners?

WEILL: We have a lot of conversations about that. We have what we call a talent-inventory process, where we spend a few days listening to our managers talk about how and what they think of people.

WSJ: What's it like to tell someone he's the runner-up?

WEILL: It is very hard. But it's a very important thing to be honest with somebody and tell somebody right off.

WSJ: What was it like when you spoke to Jamie about his departure? [Jamie Dimon, Mr. Weill's longtime protégé, was ousted as Citigroup's president not long after the merger.]

WEILL: Incredibly difficult. Because our relationship was much more than just a working relationship. Our families were friendly. I knew him growing up. He worked for me when he went to college. He came for advice when he graduated from school. It was really the only job he ever had.

It was very, very hard. Agonizingly hard. But it was something that had to be done.

WSJ: What finally convinced you to make a move?

WEILL: It was a situation that was not working as well as it might. When you have situations like that, you come to a point where something has to happen. . . . Through the merger, John Reed came to see a lot of the things I saw. . . . It was something that we did together.

WSJ: Was it harder at first to make decisions with two CEOs?

WEILL: There's no question that it is. Things happened slower.

WSJ: Does that support criticism that co-CEOs can't work?

WEILL: I am not sure that this thing would have worked from my point of view, or from Travelers' point of view, or Citicorp's point of view, had we not done it that way. . . . There have been many things that have happened since this merger where it has been fantastic that John has been here. Because he has been very, very helpful. . . . Obviously it is

---

Five Lessons from Sandy Weill on Making Mergers Work

1. Make decisions faster than you normally might, rather than slower. It will help you hold on to the good people and send the right message to everyone.
2. Treat the other company and its people with respect. Speak to people, be available, answer their questions. If people in a company believe that what you are doing is going to create a company that is going to end up being efficient and be able to grow again, I think they are much more willing to understand what's happening.
3. Use shares, options, and other methods for encouraging employee ownership, to make everyone feel part of the new company.
4. Be straightforward with people when making personnel decisions. It's very important to be honest and tell somebody your decision right off.
5. Include spouses and keep them informed. . . . It will create a family feeling. . . . The more they know about strategy, what the company is doing and what it has set out to accomplish, the more support I think you get from the whole household.

harder than having just one person. But we have to make
it work, and we had better not screw it up.

WSJ: Have you determined to leave together?

WEILL: We have no agreement to leave at the same time.

WSJ: Is there currently any process going on between you,
John, and the board to identify succession candidates?

WEILL: Not that I am aware of. We just did the deal. . . . We
have a lot of good management in this company.

WSJ: Is this Sandy Weill's last big deal?

WEILL: Who knows? . . . I certainly don't feel like I'm finished.

Daniel Vasella

CHAIRMAN AND
CHIEF EXECUTIVE
OF NOVARTIS AG

The seamless security blanket of barbed wire, barricades, and nearly a thousand Swiss police has thwarted most protesters and ruffled more than a few chief executives making their way to the 2001 World Economic Forum in Davos, Switzerland. But Daniel Vasella, the chairman and chief executive of Novartis AG, is serene upon his arrival in this Swiss ski resort. "I just flew in by helicopter. The view was just incredible," he says of the bottleneck of cars trying to force their way into town over the weekend.

The picture of his effortless arrival is deceptive. For nearly five years, Dr. Vasella has been trying to transform Novartis, the slumbering Swiss drugs giant formed by the merger of Sandoz AG and Ciba-Geigy AG in late 1996. An expanded stock-option plan, a reorganization of Novartis's research labs into smaller units, and the creation in 2000 of the Genomics Institute, a research facility in La Jolla, California, that blends an academic lab and the financial muscle of a drugs maker, are just some of the brash changes Dr. Vasella has installed. The moves could start to pay off soon. Beginning in early 2001, Novartis plans to launch about eighteen drugs for everything from diabetes to asthma to irritable-bowel syndrome. Analysts say the launches, if successful, could generate double-digit sales growth—as well as profit margins above much of the industry average—throughout much of the decade. "The launches will be important," Dr. Vasella says.

In an interview with The Wall Street Journal Europe, *Dr. Vasella talked about the lessons learned from pulling off the merger, and about Novartis's coming drug launches. He also discusses Novartis's quest to keep the innovative spirit of a small company while trying to capture the efficiencies that result from becoming a bigger concern.*

WSJ: You have said it is absolutely critical to get the coming product launches right. What marketing lessons have you learned that you are applying this time?

VASELLA: I think in some ways we haven't learned so much. This is an odd statement. What I want to say is, we already knew what we should be doing. I'm just not sure we did it.

WSJ: So what should you have been doing?

VASELLA: You need studies that are published in time, address the issue of making people aware, the right premarketing. You need to create excitement. . . . Then afterward, you need to take the big bet. You can't be halfway, do it the slow way, you know, "If it works, we'll invest more." . . . I think the organization and management is bolder than at any time in the past. If you look at the allocation of marketing and selling resources, we have way over 50 percent on the five most important growth drivers. That's a large concentration.

WSJ: What is the most important lesson you have learned in managing a company like Novartis since the merger in 1996?

VASELLA: The single most important thing is having the right people. Smart and intelligent is one thing, but it is also having people who are willing to cooperate in an organization to make it work. You need a setup where you let people work instead of blocking them. I am not even talking about a motivational environment. Just a neutral environment is already great. Because most people are motivated. You like to do your job, I like to do my job, and if people just allow us to do the job, generally we put in a lot. That is the most important thing, because they will make the right decisions. They will know much better than I what is the right technology to invest in their field.

I think one of the smartest things we probably did was setting up the Genomics Institute with Pete Schultz [the institute's director]. They are moving at a much faster speed than we anticipated—and it's him. But we put up a structure in which he can be very productive. He attracts people we couldn't have attracted to Novartis. So we needed to twist the rules a little bit and not be stubborn. They have more freedom, they can spin off some technologies, and the money flows back to the institute. There are very few constraints. I think that's a right approach.

WSJ: What is the biggest mistake you have made, then?

VASELLA: Sometimes not choosing the right people. It has probably been the most difficult part. I would say, retrospectively, I was very rigorous about being disciplined about cutting our costs and fulfilling what we promised, and, you know, that has its good parts. But at the same time, the enthusiasm for growth and the same kind of attention you should be able to put on growth wasn't there during that period. Would it have been possible to have both? I don't know if you can do it. I didn't do it. It was more sequential than parallel, what we did. . . . For example, we didn't cut a single salesperson. Quite the opposite— we increased them. There were no cost synergies in that field. But despite that, there was a loss of momentum. When you ask why, you look toward the leaders of those local businesses. In the U.S., it was unfortunate. It started badly, and we had change after change. . . . To be able to read it in time, and go, "Boom, boom, that's it, no more, this is the end now"—that is so difficult, and I certainly didn't do it then. But better late than never.

WSJ: Like at other major drug companies, alliances with smaller biotech firms play an increasingly larger role in research. How do you apply those management principles to get these alliances to work effectively?

VASELLA: Let's say you identify what you really would like [to achieve] from a point of view of technology, since there are a sea of possibilities. Then I think there are two questions. One is: Who are these people? And they must see who you are. Are we potential partners? Can we get along? Will you try to cheat each other, or do you have the perception that these are straight people? Then you have to structure a deal that is a win-win. You have to be generous, because you don't just work out the structure in order to get ink on the paper and a signature. You want them to continue to work as hard as before. The Vertex alliance is one where we have thought it through, and we have seen out of the experience that certain things work better than others. . . . There is a lot of exchange, a lot of sharing of knowledge, people going over, back and forth, and progress. There are relatively few issues.

WSJ: Are these alliances the future of pharmaceutical research?

VASELLA: It is an integral part, but I don't believe one should become hostage to it. First of all, we have seen the prices going up, the royalty rates, up-front payments—everything is going up, more expensive than a few years ago. . . . And if you go all outside, you lose the expertise inside because you don't have the people anymore to judge. You cannot have just an evaluation group that doesn't do any scientific work itself in that field. The half-life of their knowledge is only a few years.

WSJ: Will the increasing reliance on research alliances supersede or take the pressure off of the industry to consolidate further?

VASELLA: No, because when people say R&D is the main driver for the mergers, I don't believe them. It isn't the main driver. The main driver is competitive size, that they see others growing so quickly externally or internally. They get worried that they can't keep up. Or there are patent expiries ahead, where you have to manage through difficult times, and so you want to compensate for that. Or you want to strengthen the geographic presence, but you cannot do it internally. You say, "Okay, we are so weak in Japan—there is no way we can build up an organization; we need to get into an arrangement or an acquisition or whatever." But I don't believe that it is research.

It is more a question of, how can you be big and small? How can you create an environment with a spirit of small and the advantages of the economies of scale? And the larger you become, the more important this question becomes. It's like—how do you call it?—a caterpillar. You cannot become a butterfly without dramatically going through a metamorphosis. Or as with insects, once they grow, they change shape, they have to get rid of the whole carcass to change dramatically. I think the challenge one has when you go through a transformational transaction is, what is the right next shape? You can't stay in the shape of the organization you are in. You need to change.

So if, for example, we merge or buy something, I would immediately say, how can this company that we have be cut in pieces? And how could we create businesses that are large enough to have a right of existence but don't create these overall huge complexities of large organizations? And what kind of common platform do we need across all businesses that gives us economies of scale?

WSJ: What are the drivers pushing Novartis to pursue a merger or acquisition?

VASELLA: It is more the power in the marketplace. If you are in the general-practitioner market in the United States, you need thousands of people to promote. You need hundreds of millions of dollars to launch a general-practitioner product successfully. We aren't talking fifty or a hundred or two hundred, we are talking hundreds. And if you don't have the skills, you just don't make it. So size there is very relevant. And in a partnership, you won't get the assets if the potential partner doesn't believe you will leverage your assets better than anybody else in the industry, by knowledge, by reach, and by the funds you put behind it. If you are small, you just can't.

WSJ: Can you guide us where to look for the next acquisitions?

VASELLA: Yes, we would like to be bigger, but we put an even greater emphasis on performance. So if the question was performance or size, it is performance. Each and every business, as long as it is in our hands, will get all the resources needed for good ideas. We aren't constrained. . . . Take CIBA Vision [Novartis's eye-and-lens-care business]. . . . If we weren't willing to invest any more, we would sell it tomorrow, because if you don't, you destroy value.

But the highest priority is pharmaceuticals, the second-highest priority is pharmaceuticals, the third-highest priority is pharmaceuticals. I would say we are first a health-care company. Within health care, we are a drug company, not a diagnostics company and not a device company. Besides drugs, we have two businesses: CIBA Vision and the nutrition business, which is doing very well but [isn't] in the core portfolio. So, if somebody came and said, "Would you like to swap? We have some kind of business that is too small to remain in pharmaceuticals, and we would like to become stronger in that area," we would say, "Sure."

Part Three

Building
a Brand

Tina Brown

CHAIRMAN
AND EDITOR
IN CHIEF OF
TALK MAGAZINE

When Tina Brown was editor of Vanity Fair, *she pushed celebrity journalism to a new limit when she put Demi Moore nude and pregnant on the cover. At* The New Yorker, *she created a stir with a long story about a dominatrix. Both magazines are owned by Condé Nast, a unit of Advance Publications, Inc.*

Throughout her controversial career, her fans and her harshest critics have agreed on one thing: She has an unusual gift for making a splash and getting people to talk about her products. In 1999, as she prepared to launch a new magazine called Talk, *with The Walt Disney Co.'s Miramax Films, she took a break to discuss the art of standing out in a crowded marketplace.*

WSJ: You are called the queen of buzz. What is your view on that?

BROWN: I am not sure what that means. I tend to think that "buzz" has become a pejorative word that people think can be grafted onto a publication by some sort of machine. . . . Buzz is reader interest. And if you produce a magazine that is interesting to readers, then I suppose it has buzz. . . .

I think any good magazine represents the most interesting stories you had at the time you went to press. . . . Right up to the last minute. And the weaker things don't make the cut. . . . Now, if what interests me sort of turns on a lot of other people, too, then so much the better. But it usually gets selected for that reason, as opposed to "Is this about buzz?"

WSJ: So you trust your instincts?

BROWN: Yes, I do. I'm easily bored.

WSJ: What were some of the things you did to sustain interest in your magazines? For instance, what was the most daring thing you did at *The New Yorker*?

BROWN: At *The New Yorker*, one thing we did that broke with tradition was the special edition on the Princess of Wales's death. She died on Saturday night, and we had a special issue out for the next Friday. . . . When I first came in . . . the magazine was not set up to do that. . . . It was very much a magazine that was a literary culture. We did something that was very journalistic . . . and we performed like a news magazine but kept our literary standards. . . .

The New Yorker was a weekly magazine that wasn't using its frequency in any way. It was performing as a monthly or even a quarterly. It was a very bad syndrome to have the magazine piling up next to readers' beds. Very self-destructive.

I always saw the news as the way to grow readers. . . . We had to have one or two pieces a week which absolutely were the topic of interest in terms of what people wanted to see that particular week. Those topics were a necessary seduction point. Then readers could be seduced further by other stories once they were in the magazine.

WSJ: And at *Vanity Fair*?

BROWN: The riskiest thing at *Vanity Fair* was to put Demi Moore naked and pregnant on the cover. Originally, we had wanted to photograph around the fact that she was pregnant. But then, at the end of the shoot, Annie Leibovitz took the picture she really wanted to take. She came back to me and said, "Do you think we could ever use this in the magazine?" I said, "Let's put it on the cover." I'd recently had a baby myself, and I felt incredible affinity with the pride that she showed with her pregnant stomach.

WSJ: There are so many magazines out there. How do you define who you are and get attention?

BROWN: I have always felt that you should be able to throw a magazine on the floor at any page and know whose magazine it is. If you think about *The New Yorker*, for instance, that typeface is unmistakable. You just put it on the floor, and there is a cartoon, there is the typeface. The same is true of *Vanity Fair* at this point. . . . So I really wanted to create a look that everybody knew immediately was *Talk* magazine. . . . And a very strong point of view. I think that doing bits and pieces of everybody else's publication is not going to help you.

WSJ: Is it important to make people who read it feel special?

BROWN: I spend a lot of time on cover lines, captions. I think everything about the page should work to get you in. . . . I do a tremendous amount of sending them back if they are not right. . . . Blurbs, the captions, the quotes that are pulled out, the contents page. All these little bits and pieces are about the atmosphere and tone of the magazine, which should invite you in. . . . The page should have attitude. It should have a relationship. It shouldn't just be something that could just be anywhere. . . .

In the new magazine, an emergency-room doctor is keeping a diary and we are publishing it untouched. It's a description of a particular medical emergency. . . . My editors found him and brought him in, and at first, nothing we talked about made him light up. Finally I asked him, "Do you keep a diary?" And he said, "Well, yes, I do." You get that often in letters or e-mails or diaries—voices come out that won't otherwise.

WSJ: How important is a launch party?

BROWN: This is a very busy and competitive marketplace. So I think that a launch needs all the help it can get. . . . It is a very big country. You have to reach a lot of people. It is a new thing. I think the more you can persuade people to go out and buy that first issue, the more you can achieve success.

WSJ: Is any publicity good publicity?

BROWN: Publicity is different than discussion. When I think of the word "publicity," I see a press agent who goes out and generates attention. Discussion about a magazine is very, very important. In a busy world, a magazine must compel the readers. . . .

What I've always looked for and felt that I can deliver is reader engagement. People are rarely indifferent to the magazines I've put out. Sometimes they hate it, but they are engaged.

WSJ: You have to spend a lot of money to pay for a launch.

BROWN: I have much less of a budget to work with than I did at Condé Nast. . . . I had to be much more resourceful.

One thing I learned at *Tatler* was that if you don't have a budget, you have to have a point of view. Because you can't send fifteen people to cover the story. You better have a completely different interpretation of the story, and then people will pay attention to it.

WSJ: If you did something else besides editing a magazine, what would it be?

BROWN: I would probably run a theater. . . . If I could be re-incarnated and have another go. . . . I think the excitement of a live audience is fantastic. I love audience response in that sense, in terms of the way it changes night after night.

WSJ: What products do you admire?

BROWN: The Bug . . . the [Volkswagen] Bug was great. . . .

Now that I am a partner with a movie company, I find it very inspiring to see what tremendous imagination the movie companies bring to the launch of everything. They have a new product six and ten times a year. There is nothing similar between one product and the next except a sort of system of the publication. But they have to reinvent the wheel each time.

WSJ: Is it more challenging to shake up an established entity like *The New Yorker* or to create something from scratch like *Talk?*

BROWN: At *The New Yorker,* [my job] was all about management. There was a big staff, and I hired thirty-two editors and writers and let over sixty people go. That was an enormous, taxing management challenge.

I had to rethink a very established brand. . . . But I always recognized that [*The New Yorker*] was a creative template that could not be pushed too far. It was something I wished to preserve, and I didn't wish to completely alter it. Because I felt that would interfere with the . . . DNA of the magazine. So I think had I stayed, I would have found the restraints increasingly frustrating. . . .

Here I've had no institutional responsibility. It has been very fun and stimulating putting a staff together and hunting them down. Figuring out if they are complementary under pressure. . . . But there were these other problems, which is that you don't [yet] know what [the magazine] is, either. So that became quite difficult over time, because you would try to persuade people, for instance, to do an interview for a magazine that doesn't exist.

WSJ: You are very identified with the magazines you have worked with. There aren't that many editors who are as well-known as you. Has that helped or hurt your product?

BROWN: I've edited three magazines now, and I think there are a large number of readers who have read them. And if they enjoy them, then maybe they'll read the next one. So perhaps I've developed some kind of reader interest. . . .

Five Lessons from Tina Brown on Marketing

1. Trust your instincts. I will listen to anybody . . . but I usually come to my senses and try to get back in touch with what I initially thought.
2. Have a strong visual identity. . . . Doing bits and pieces of everybody else . . . isn't going to help you.
3. Throw a party. A launch needs all the help it can get. It is a big country. You have to reach a lot of people.
4. Be creative with spending. Find new talent and package your product in a different way.

   If you don't have a [large] budget you have to have a point of view.
5. Utilize your existing talent in different ways. With writers, for instance . . . the trick is finding what turns them on . . . making them feel they can write about topics they couldn't before.

I think it can be an advantage to the magazine. It is probably helpful in a crowded marketplace—not to have to explain as much about the editor. But I think that [editors] are only as good as the last magazine they put out. . . . People are not interested if the magazine is not interesting. . . . You can get people to look, but you can't get people to come back.

Ian Schrager

FOUNDER AND
CHAIRMAN OF
IAN SCHRAGER
HOTELS, LLC

On any given night, guests at Ian Schrager's hotels range from high-maintenance celebrities wanting VIP treatment to business travelers who require only a dinner reservation and a good night's sleep.

Catering to both the elite and the masses simultaneously—without offending either group—is the daily challenge Mr. Schrager confronts with his booming boutique properties, which range from the Royalton in New York to the Sanderson in London. While corporate travelers make up 35 percent of Mr. Schrager's guests, it is the continual flow of models, actors, and media titans that gives his spots buzz. Deciding who gets special treatment is an art that "separates the men from the boys," Mr. Schrager says. It is also a skill required in many fickle industries, from restaurants and retail to night-clubs and resorts.

The colorful hotelier, who ran the fabled Studio 54 night-club and was later jailed for tax evasion, says his hotels, with their popular bars and restaurants, aren't for everyone. Guest rooms often lack corporate amenities such as fax machines—"they're too institutional"—and hotel design is quirky: Elevators at St. Martins Lane in London sport video screens with images of human eyeballs.

Mr. Schrager's insistence that his hotels look and feel a certain way has, at times, proved thorny. In August 2000, his Mondrian hotel in Los Angeles agreed to pay $1 million to settle a discrimination suit brought by nine former bellmen who claimed they were fired because Mr. Schrager thought they were "too ethnic." The hotelier says he doesn't discriminate and that the problem was the bellmen couldn't speak English and wore "too many tattoos," among other things.

By the summer of 2002, Mr. Schrager will have opened another seven properties, giving him a total of fourteen branded hotels worldwide. The Wall Street Journal *checked in with the hotelier in August 2000 to learn how he manages his very different groups of clientele.*

WSJ: How do you balance being provocative with providing the basics, like getting hot food to the room on time?

SCHRAGER: Well, that's the trick. Everyone thinks that only people who wear black and live in SoHo come to my hotels. No. That is not the case. . . . If you don't have corporate business, you don't have any business. . . . But you see, it is sort of a new definition of service. It is not one based upon efficiency of execution, like Marriott's, which is state-of-the-art. . . . It is something more based upon the experience, and because the experience is so unique and so elevating . . . perhaps you are a little bit more tolerant of certain things.

WSJ: Such as?

SCHRAGER: Perhaps you are willing to suffer not having enough shelf space by the bed because the piece next to the bed really looks good, really looks cool, and you have never seen it before. And, boy, you must be a member of this special club that is in this hotel. Therefore, if you don't have twenty-four-inch by twenty-four-inch shelf space, which some rubric says you are supposed to have, it is okay. . . . In the interest of being on the edge and being provocative, you have to take risks. . . .

There are businesspeople, I think, like myself, that really want to be a part of this sophisticated scene. And they have to deal with or accept maybe a desk that is only eighteen inches wide and maybe not quite long enough. The reason that the lighting is not as bright as it should be is because I want everyone to look good. . . .

WSJ: How do you accommodate the businessman who wants to have a drink after work but can't find a place to sit because the hotel bar is so popular?

SCHRAGER: We make great effort to get away from that by making different entrances and security and all that kind of thing. . . . I don't like a place where the person walking into the hotel and checking in and going up into the elevator feels disenfranchised, feels he is walking into the middle of a nightclub. . . .

However . . . not being able to get into a bar, and not being able to get seated in a restaurant right away—although I don't love that—that is what you would experience if you went to the hottest restaurant or bar in that city. And why don't you want to go to the hottest bar and restaurant that is right downstairs?

WSJ: How do you protect your bars and restaurants from being overtaken by people who aren't staying at the hotel? For instance, what about groups of guys who come to your bars to meet women?

SCHRAGER: We don't permit that. . . . There's no nice way to say no to anyone. You might say it's too crowded. . . . We've tried everything and we are still working on that by reservations lists, by priority lists and privilege cards. It is just a difficult process.

I just wish there was an editing process that somebody would come up with . . . that is not so demeaning. . . . You like to have a woman be able to go into a bar and have a drink and listen to the music and not be afraid she is going to be accosted or bothered by men trying to pick her up. . . . There is no way not to make mistakes because it is a very intuitive, impulsive process. . . .

Look, when you have a private dinner party at your home, you exercise the same judgment. You try and invite people who are going to get along, that are not going to be dead weight, that are not going to be obnoxious. If you have a person who doesn't talk very much, you might sit that person next to somebody who is very sweet-talking. It is that kind of procedure. But for some reason, when it makes its way into the public domain it takes on an aura of obnoxiousness. . . .

WSJ: Are you ever worried about the legalities of turning people away?

SCHRAGER: It's not the kind of thing it was with Studio 54. The door policy there got a lot of people aggravated. It's not the same screening process. All hotel guests are guaranteed admission.

WSJ: So how do you know who's staying there?

SCHRAGER: The reservation list. . . . Sometimes people will buy hotel rooms just to get into the bars and restaurant. . . . Sometimes people will buy a hotel room and they will try and get ten or twenty people in and pass the key. We figure that out.

WSJ: How important is the person working at the door of your hotels' bars and restaurants?

SCHRAGER: The doorman has to sort of understand and be part of that scene. . . . What makes it the hot bar? It is not the music, because everybody has the same music. And it is not the liquor. . . . [It's] the people that go there. And so how does that all happen? . . . There is an editing process. . . . And we have door people who do that.

WSJ: Your Mondrian hotel just settled a discrimination suit brought by nine former bellmen who claimed they were fired for being "too ethnic."

SCHRAGER: Having the right look of a hotel has nothing to do with race or nationality. Our staff is diverse; over 50 percent of the people working for me are minorities. But if someone puts down a cup of coffee, and there is a tattoo on every finger, that is inappropriate. It was a handwritten memo to myself [where the words "too ethnic" were used] and it was unfortunate. It's not the way I feel in my heart.

WSJ: How do you give celebrities a sense of privacy?

SCHRAGER: Well, if it is a cool place, the people won't gawk, because it is not cool to gawk. And they won't go over and ask for autographs. . . .

Seating people in the restaurant is an art. . . . There's a real hierarchy with the tables. . . . What are the important tables? Who sits there and who gets that? And where do you see good-looking people? . . . You try and make an exciting visual tableau. . . . That is something that separates the men from the boys. I don't know if this is a good example. But it is almost like someone who carries money in their pocket and puts the big bills on the outside and the little bills on the inside. . . .

I know that with the Royalton, for instance, we have a whole row of banquettes. They are made like big, luxurious, comfortable couches in the room. And those are where the celebrities sit. And by the way, the most important celebrity sits at table one and the hierarchy goes back to table six.

WSJ: So two businessmen walk in who are staying at your hotel. They are nicely dressed, but they are not with women. They are not celebrities. Where do you seat them?

SCHRAGER: We would put them in some place that might not be as visible as where we would put a celebrity. I wouldn't put them in Siberia, necessarily. . . . And it is flexible. . . . When I got started in Studio 54 with Steve [Rubell], we didn't want it to ever be too gay, and we never wanted it to be too straight. And we didn't want it to be too many women, or too many men. It is a bouillabaisse, it's a mix.

WSJ: What does someone who is a VIP care about that someone who is the average businessperson doesn't care about?

SCHRAGER: They want to be fawned over, plain and simple. . . . We have all these [categories]—VIP Royal, VIP Super Royal.

WSJ: Who is a Super Royal VIP?

SCHRAGER: Someone who to me is a particular thrill that they are in my hotel, and I really don't want to leave anything to chance. I want to make sure, without being obsequious, that we are taking care of them.

WSJ: Is the chairman of Nike a Super Royal VIP?

SCHRAGER: Yes.

WSJ: Leonardo DiCaprio?

SCHRAGER: No. For me . . . I don't mean to be unkind . . . to me it is so funny. . . . If I was in the nightclub business now, all the bank presidents would get in instead of people that got in before. I think, I forget his name now, Phil [Knight], the guy from Nike, I think that guy is brilliant. Iconoclastic.

WSJ: What could you do for him in a hotel that would make his stay special?

Schrager: There is a certain restraint involved. But to let him know we are here. Whatever it is you want, whatever, we will get it for you. Suit of armor at four in the morning— no problem, you've got it.

WSJ: How do you prevent guests from taking advantage of your hospitality?

SCHRAGER: We are in the hospitality business. There's nothing we wouldn't do for our guests. Nothing legal we wouldn't do.

WSJ: Rates for your new Henry Hudson hotel, opening in New York this fall [of 2000], will start at ninety-five dollars per night. Do you worry such a low price will attract a different crowd for your hotels? Such as bus tours?

SCHRAGER: That is not a segment we go after. It is part of the wholesale business. You don't say no to the buses. You just don't go after that business.

WSJ: Do you think people know which hotel they should be in?

SCHRAGER: To a certain extent . . . I think there is a sort of self-operative editing process.

WSJ: How do you deal with people who don't like the details of some hotels—say, the cone-shaped stainless-steel sinks or a single green apple mounted on the wall?

SCHRAGER: I don't feel that they are wrong. . . . I am looking to get people to notice my hotels. . . . I was in an elevator in our Paramount hotel, where you have different colors for the elevators, and somebody said, "This is the hotel from hell." And I am right in the elevator. To me, they don't like this hotel. That hotel makes $24 million a year. Bottom line.

Kevin J. Roberts

CHIEF EXECUTIVE
OF SAATCHI &
SAATCHI PLC

It's hard to believe now, but not too long ago tech-savvy doomsayers were confidently predicting that the Internet would destroy the traditional advertising and media world.

They're still predicting, but the reality is turning out to be a lot more complicated—at least for now. Ad agencies, television networks, and even newspapers are enjoying their best years in history, thanks in part to the billions of dollars that Internet start-ups have spent on old-media ads. At the same time, advertisers are struggling to make the Internet work as an advertising medium. The percentage of consumers responding to Internet ads by clicking on them has plummeted—and some of Silicon Valley's biggest kingpins barely advertise on the Web at all.

*Internet advertising that works has become the industry's
Holy Grail. Now, major old-line ad agencies are finally join-
ing the hunt, bringing a different perspective. Leading one
such agency is New Zealander Kevin J. Roberts, the energetic
chief executive of Saatchi & Saatchi PLC, the London agency
with seven thousand employees in ninety-two countries
around the world.*

*A former rugby player known for sometimes expressing
himself in brash ways—he once fired a gun at a Coke vending
machine during his days as an executive at PepsiCo, Inc.—
Mr. Roberts isn't one to hold back. Visiting San Francisco to
address @d:tech, an Internet advertising conference held in
2000, he shared his views on the future of the Internet and
what his daughter's car says about Web advertising.*

WSJ: We've seen the boom in dot-com ad spending, then the
collapse of some dot-coms in the last few months. What
went wrong and where is the Internet headed?

ROBERTS: Candace Carpenter of iVillage joined our board,
which is a measure of my belief the Internet is here to stay.
But guess what? A lot of players are disappearing, and only
the smart guys are cutting it. No s—, Sherlock. . . . The
Internet isn't going away, but the easy bucks have gone
down the toilet. A lot of bad ideas benefited from [the dot-
com boom].

I was speaking with some guys from Harvard recently,
and do you know that two thirds of the MBA class are
going to dot-coms? I told them they were nuts. . . .

No medium has ever replaced another. It isn't an either-
or situation. There's a new way of communicating, and the

challenge is how to bring emotion and engagement—how to bring love—to a personal and sometimes antisocial medium. For me, [the Internet] is like electricity. I don't care where it came from, or how it got there. I just want to figure out how to emotionally connect with it.

WSJ: What makes you think one medium won't replace another?

ROBERTS: It all started with newspapers. Guess what? They're still here. . . . Wasn't television supposed to replace radio? Now there are more radio stations than ever before. Now people tell me that the Internet will replace television. They're smoking dope. It isn't going to happen. It isn't going to go away.

WSJ: Everyone is pretty much in agreement that online advertising isn't working. What is it going to take to make it work?

ROBERTS: Now it looks like hamburger meat. The advertising all stinks. It's so boring. Remember the old 1950s ads on television? That's what it looks like. . . .

Agencies have got to endorse [the Internet], but the problem is you've got a lot of forty- and fifty-year-old guys at agencies who are threatened by it. So they create separate groups and hire bleached-blond skateboarders to deal with it. It's bulls—. Consumers see this as part of their daily intake of communication. . . .

You'll see a transition [on the Internet] from information to relationships. Great brands can't exist just by providing information. The great ones have mystery and sensuality. Our task is to create mystery and sensuality on the Internet. Right now we're failing hopelessly, just hopelessly. . . .

Look at two successful brands. Apple is the most sensual product since the vibrator. It's built on sensuality. My daughter just got a new [Volkswagen] Beetle, and every day she talks to it. It's a member of our family who happens to live in the garage because she can't fit it in her bedroom. She almost strokes it. We live in New Zealand, and people stop to take pictures of it. People want to pat it. That's what we're going to create with the Internet.

WSJ: Despite the recent drop in the market, there are still some online advertising agencies rattling their sabers, saying they are going to acquire traditional agencies. After all, online shops do get higher multiples in the stock market.

ROBERTS: That's absolutely nuts. John Chambers of Cisco talks about "co-opetition." Why don't we all try to do what we're good at? These guys are great at technology, taking it places it's never been before. Let's go on dates—not get married.

WSJ: What impact is the recent downturn in tech stocks having on ad agencies? Isn't the downfall of the dot-coms eventually going to hurt?

ROBERTS: Everybody's realized it's about building brands, and everyone is investing in that. I feel bullish about the next three to four years. The old economy is roaring back. P&G won't take losing $57 billion in stock [market value] lying down. . . . The global ad agencies will do better and better, although some of the smaller shops may get hurt. . . .

One of the biggest things that's going to happen is a lot of people are going to come back from dot-coms bruised,

Five Lessons from Kevin Roberts on Advertising and the Web

1. Remember that no medium has ever replaced another. It isn't either-or. Newspapers and radio survived the arrival of TV, and TV will survive the coming of the Internet.

2. Great brands are about relationships, not just information. Internet advertising must have mystery and sensuality.

3. Online agencies and old-line agencies should do what they are good at. They should go on dates—not get married.

4. Welcome back the kids who defected to dot-coms. They'll come back wounded but smarter.

5. Stop obsessing about technology and start obsessing about ideas. The "e" doesn't stand for electronic; it stands for emotion.

battered, shaken up, and broke, their options not worth a box of Charmin. . . . I was excited to see kids doing the dot-com thing. But to think they would all succeed would have been ridiculous. Now they'll come back wounded, smarter, and with a little scar tissue, which is a good thing.

WSJ: One of the best ideas I've heard was from former creative directors at TBWA / Chiat / Day talking about what they could do online with the Energizer Bunny.

ROBERTS: Most clients aren't thinking like that. Neither are the agencies. . . . These cowboys are obsessed with technology instead of ideas. They think "e" stands for electronic, when "e" stands for emotion. That's where they're missing it.

Part Four

*Learning
from the
New Economy*

Michael Dell

CHAIRMAN AND
CEO OF
DELL COMPUTER
CORPORATION

What Henry Ford did to the car business with his mass-production system for the Model T, Michael S. Dell did to the personal-computer business with the Internet. The stunning success Dell Computer Corporation has achieved by taking consumer orders online and then orchestrating production tailored to each customer has made Mr. Dell a star on Wall Street—and a guru in Detroit, where Henry Ford's successors are courting him for advice on how to make their businesses look like his.

Why would a huge automaker seek Mr. Dell's advice? Because Dell Computer's ultrafast build-to-order approach—which allows the company to put a customer's money in the bank before it pays for parts and labor—generates 160 percent return on invested capital, not to mention stock valuations a Detroit chief executive officer can only dream about.

A personal friend of Ford CEO Jacques Nasser and a frequent speaker on the impact of the Internet on manufacturing, Mr. Dell has his own interests in the auto business, including an investment in CarsDirect.com, an online automobile dealer. Auto companies have long relied on having large stocks of vehicles on hand, and auto dealers have vigorously opposed moves to allow consumers to order directly from the factory via the Web, bypassing the traditional sales channel.

But in a 1999 interview, Mr. Dell talked about how car makers can use the Internet to streamline procurement and to reshape service and sales.

WSJ: How can what you've done at Dell Computer to embrace the Internet apply to the auto industry?

DELL: One of the big changes that is brought about by information technology is that the cost of connections and linkages has gone down dramatically. So if you've got an operation that builds a component, the cost to communicate with that operation in an information sense, if it is done electronically, goes to zero. That means you can build a linkage between a components supplier and a manufacturer and make it very, very efficient.

That enables you to scale more quickly, gives you more flexibility, you can manage supplier networks in a more dynamic fashion, and get things off your balance sheet that aren't your specialty—and companies can really home in on something that they're really great at.

WSJ: And you don't have to own it.

DELL: You don't have to own it. And a company can really become an expert in one thing. . . .

We have roughly thirty thousand employees now, and $26 billion in revenue this year. If we were vertically integrated, I don't know how many employees we'd have, but it would be some huge number. And we wouldn't be a fifteen-year-old company. There's no way you can build a company like that in fifteen years if you had to do it all yourself. So [information technology] creates speed, it creates flexibility.

The other thing that kind of pops out in this is the amount of assets that are tied up [in the old system]. . . . So the biggest item on the balance sheet of these car manufacturers is inventory. . . . It's not just their inventory, it's the dealer inventory, it's the in-transit inventory, it's inventory anywhere in the system, from the components all the way through to the end customer. Even the spare-parts inventory and all that stuff.

WSJ: The auto companies have built their business models on having it—the instant sale. You walk in the dealership, there's a car. They get paid when a car comes off the assembly line. Don't they have to redo their whole business culture?

DELL: They have to start accelerating the pace of change in the company and preconditioning people that things are going to change. This is what Jacques Nasser and others are trying to do.

WSJ: Which end of the rope do you pull first?

DELL: My guess would be that they could have quick hits and improvements on their supplier side. . . . If we tell our suppliers, "Hey, look, you need to deliver at six-twenty in the morning, and you got to come to this dock, and it's got to be this many boxes and has to be this high," they say, "Yes, sir. You're buying a billion dollars' worth of stuff from us, we'll do it. No problem."

WSJ: Did you have to use carrots to get people to start communicating with you electronically? Did you have to cull suppliers that weren't making the grade?

DELL: When we were much smaller, some of them said, "Well, we're not going to do that." We had some pretty convincing arguments. For one, we could legitimately say if you weren't selling to Dell, you were losing market share. And it was true, because we were growing much faster than any competitor. So the vast majority of them said, "Okay, we'll play this game." The ones that did it great got more business, and the ones that didn't got less business or no business.

WSJ: Were there specific tools other than rewards, or the stick, to enable suppliers to do it your way?

DELL: We had supplier conferences. . . . We had supplier report cards. We created valuechain.dell.com, which is an internal site that only suppliers and Dell have access to that took the supplier report card online so they knew how they were doing. And we just made it a relentless focus.

WSJ: Was it the technology that was the most difficult, or people?

DELL: I think the suppliers in our industry were . . . used to a high rate of change for things around them in general. Whether it's distribution channels or technologies, this didn't seem to be that big of a deal for them. I'm talking about the successful ones. I don't know that I have a good case for the not-successful ones, because we didn't really pay much attention to them.

WSJ: How do you measure supplier performance?

DELL: We asked our procurement teams to act as almost an extension of the supplier and to get involved in operations, understanding that supplier, and understanding the products and commodities. We go really, really deep into understanding these things: What are the materials involved? Where do they all come from?

WSJ: Do you think the automakers have the same kind of involvement with their suppliers?

DELL: I don't have a good handle on that. It was absolutely critical for us. The advantage for us was we didn't have two hundred suppliers to do this. We really narrowed it down, and said we're going to focus, we're going to have twenty-five suppliers supply 85 percent of our stuff.

WSJ: When can you click on the screen to view a car and say, "What does the red exterior with the gold interior look like?"

DELL: You can do that now. Is it good enough? That's a work-in-progress question. . . . Most Web sites today have not appropriately anticipated the availability of broadband information—which is starting to happen. . . .

By and large today, you're showing more like a photo-quality rendition, and you can see information about something you already have familiarity with. Are you going to introduce a completely new model that nobody's ever seen? . . . I'm not convinced that's going to happen just yet.

But you've got to remember that this [technology] really changes quickly. Five years ago, if you asked eighteen-to-twenty-five-year-olds, "How many of you will buy books online?" I think, like, 94 percent of them would have said they're not going to do it. Now, of course, 94 percent say, "Absolutely . . . that's the only way to buy books."

WSJ: You're involved with CarsDirect. In less than one year, CarsDirect has shown you can do a great deal of the purchase process of a car online, whereas two years ago you had a lot of people saying, "Oh no, no."

DELL: "Involved" might be a strong word. I'm familiar with it. . . . The consumer has better information, you have transparency of pricing. You can't trick the consumer anymore. The businesses that had an advantage because they sold things in a geographic area where people had limited information, and they couldn't travel to go buy something else . . . are in real trouble.

WSJ: How do you resolve the issue of channel conflict—where you've got an installed base of dealers who feel like they've got rights to defend? There was a brief episode in your company where you had dealers, and now you don't.

DELL: It was a small portion of our sales. Fortunately.

WSJ: How did you unwind that?

DELL: Virtually all [car] sales are through dealers. One thing is already starting to happen . . . the profit of the dealer is moving away from the car and toward the service—which, for the car companies, opens up a real opportunity. . . . You are the service network. You're not the sales network.

WSJ: When you started in Internet direct selling, did you do something that you considered ultimately to be a mistake, and how did you fix it?

DELL: Just like the starting of the company, any mistake you make, in hindsight, looks to be so insignificant. You just go change it. That's one of the beauties of the Internet. You can experiment with things so easily. . . .

When we started with transactions, the first thing we had was an online order status. This is before you could even order a computer [online]. We didn't know how many people would use this thing. We built a link from the Internet to our core system so you could get order status instantly. . . . You called up and went to dell.com, which was still in its infancy, and one of the main things was "Order Status." It turns out we had five thousand people . . . in the first four days, and it went straight up from there. What this was telling us was . . . people want this. . . . And then we started improving it.

We sent this team off and said, "You guys go figure out how to get information from UPS, and Airborne, and FedEx, and integrate this whole thing." I want somebody to be able to go online and find exactly where their computer is, minute by minute. . . . It's self-service. The customer is now going [to the website], and they're not calling us on the phone. This poor person whose job it is to read things off a screen and tell a customer what the screen says, that's not a very value-added job. Now that person can go do something else.

WSJ: Does the auto industry focus on the supply chain or the chain to the customer?

Five Lessons from Michael Dell on
How to Build a Better Car

1. Use the Internet to lower the cost of developing links between manufacturers and suppliers, manufacturers and dealers.
2. Turn over to outsiders operations that aren't central to the business.
3. Accelerate the pace of change, and condition employees to accept change.
4. Experiment with Internet businesses. Develop trials to see what happens when customers can access information in ways they never could before.
5. Consider what to do with the investment that could be freed up by shedding inventory and other assets now on the balance sheet.

DELL: They seem to be interested in the supply chain and the manufacturing process. For us to build a PC, it's three to four hours or something like this. A lot of traditional manufacturing people find that amazing. It's the way we design the process: Take out touches, take out time, and have the whole thing customized. The automotive industry is one where the interest level is among the highest.

WSJ: How do you get the key people in a company to make the kinds of changes you're talking about?

DELL: It might be tutorials, it might be forcing it on them. We . . . moved all of our internal [human resources] systems to the Web. If you were a manager, you couldn't do anything unless you did it on our intranet. You couldn't hire somebody, you couldn't fire somebody, you couldn't give them a raise, couldn't give them stock options. Nothing could happen unless you did it online.

John Roth

PRESIDENT AND
CHIEF EXECUTIVE
OF NORTEL
NETWORKS
CORPORATION

Few business problems are more challenging than transforming an Old Economy culture to meet the demands of the New Economy. And few big companies have gotten more kudos for doing so than Nortel Networks Corp. Indeed, Bear Stearns dubbed the Canadian company the "poster boy" for companies making the transition into the New Economy.

Now discussions about a potential $100 billion sale of Nortel's optical components division to Corning, Inc., could produce the company's biggest payoff yet. A deal is by no means certain, but the two are talking about combining their optical components operations in an arrangement that could give Nortel a major stake in Corning or the combined operations.

Big transactions and fast changes are a hallmark of Nortel, which was founded in 1895. For decades, its core business was supplying switches and other gear used in traditional voice telecommunications networks. But lately, it has been riding a growth wave because of surging sales of high-capacity fiber-optic systems that transmit digital data through the Internet, plus increased sales of other networking gear.

Nortel used to develop most of its equipment in-house. But the company has spent more than $11 billion in nine months to buy a slew of technology companies. It also acquired California's Bay Networks in a $7 billion deal.

Nortel's president and chief executive, John Roth, has pinned the company's hopes squarely on Internet technology since he took office in 1997. So far the strategy is pleasing investors: Nortel's stock is up fivefold since the start of 1999. In a 2000 interview, he discussed his strategy:

WSJ: You've described the changes at Nortel as a "right-angle turn." When did you decide the company needed a sudden refocusing?

ROTH: In the fall of 1997 it became really clear that we needed to make a big shift, and I mean *big shift.* What was absolutely clear to me was that the Internet was well accepted in the marketplace, that the Internet protocol was becoming standardized. And what it meant is that networks are going to move from being based on [telephone] technology to [Internet] technology.

I sent an e-mail to a group of sixty thousand employees at the time, and I described what I call the right-angle turn toward "Web tone." The opportunity for Nortel is to build the Web into something that is as pervasive and as reliable and as just plain taken for granted as dial tone. Everybody has to have a telephone. Everybody having access to the Web is going to hit that point in society at some time.

That was the vision. It addressed the issue of what the portfolio has to be, but it also touched on the isssue of what the culture had to become, one where we really valued time above all else. Time and speed.

WSJ: What would have happened if you hadn't made the changes?

ROTH: We would have looked like some of our competitors.

WSJ: Which is?

ROTH: Not as interesting. Look at our market cap compared with our competitors. When we went down this path, when it was announced I would be CEO of this corporation, our market cap was $22 billion. We're now sitting around $200 billion. . . . A lot of those guys now would actually be easy acquisition targets for Nortel if they made sense for us.

WSJ: How do you get a big, old company to move "at Web speed," as you like to say?

ROTH: It's very tough. I remember meeting with the management team about the changes we were going to make, and I wasn't exactly getting the buy-in I wanted. I said, "Look, guys, it's easier to build a new company than to turn an old one around." It took a tremendous force of will to get the organization to start to change.

WSJ: What did you talk about with these guys?

ROTH: How we would move quickly. At the time we started, just to give you some examples, to approve an R&D project in this corporation required agreement from the board of directors. We'd see forms with fifteen signatures on them, and then they'd go to the board of directors to get their signatures. We don't have time for that.

Our attitude towards acquisitions: We'd look at a start-up and people would come back and say, "You know, pretty hot stuff, but we can do better. We shouldn't buy them; we'll just design something better." I had R&D projects that were five years old and still hadn't hit the market.

I assembled what we call the CEO Forum. We picked seventy-five people, three teams of twenty-five, from the rank and file of Nortel. We got people at every level who were nominated by their peers, people they'd follow and respect. Everybody got together, no name tags, no badges, no titles. . . . It was a huge event because a whole bunch of vice presidents were not invited to this forum—and they saw engineers being invited who hadn't been with the company for six months. It was quite a turning event in the sense of culture.

WSJ: What did you learn from the CEO Forum?

ROTH: A lot of great ideas came out. Our whole outsourcing initiative came out of that workshop. A whole different approach to managing our research-and-development programs came out of that. Faster, quicker, more in tune with the marketplace. . .

The outsourcing led to the closure of, what, we're down to six plants from twenty-four. We got rid of eighteen plants. We've now outsourced 50 percent of our circuit-board production.

WSJ: Is it saving money?

ROTH: Absolutely, and it's making us agile. You look right now:
I have to ramp my optical [manufacturing capacity] by an
order of magnitude. Well it turns out that 75 percent of my
optical is now being made by outsourcers. They're five times
bigger than I am. So what looks like 100 percent to me looks
like 20 percent to them. They can handle 20 percent. My
team would really struggle to do 100 percent. And then we
were able to focus on those things that only we can do. . . .

We tore up a whole bunch of sacred cows and didn't
replace them with anything. It created a huge void in a
whole bunch of areas because Nortel was a company that
followed procedures with great diligence, and suddenly I
pulled away a whole bunch of procedures and said, "You
can't follow those anymore."

WSJ: Any examples of what procedures you got rid of?

ROTH: The biggest one was we had a series of what were
called gate reviews. They were reviews on R&D projects
that took place during various stages of the project. Originally these reviews were quite simple, but over a fifteen-
year period they became terribly complex and very
bureaucratic.

WSJ: What is the new R&D process?

ROTH: It's called the portfolio management team. A team gets
together, they meet every Monday, and they make decisions about what are the priorities for the team this week.
That's a huge change. Before, we used to look at these
things once every eight months and make decisions.

It used to be that things lasted five years, some of these
projects. We would set the goals, and we would work for

five years toward that destination in the certainty that what we predicted five years earlier was correct. Well, in five years the Internet happened, and here we're still working on the same project!

WSJ: How long does a typical project take now?

ROTH: Around a year, year-plus. There are some that are longer-term than that, but we've broken them into chunks, like, let's get the fundamental technology working and then we'll add the features and functionality later.

WSJ: How did the acquisition of Bay Networks help shake up the corporate culture?

ROTH: We adopted many of the practices of Bay into Nortel. Nortel was very much a hierarchical structure. Information rose a level at a time. Decisions often were made several levels above where the information resided. We took a lot of that out. . . .

Stock options was probably one of the most significant changes we made. We had never as a company given stock options as deeply into the organization as Bay did. There's basically nobody who's ineligible to get a stock option [now]. The attention to the success of the company that that gives is fabulous. We would never have predicted what a powerful force it is, but the Bay philosophy taught us that.

WSJ: What obstacles did you run into in making changes?

ROTH: A lot of resistance to change in any form. Big loss of entitlement for some people. General managers not wanting to part with their factories. So what happened is we changed some of the individuals. A lot of individuals changed, because either they had to be part of the program or they couldn't be part of Nortel.

We had a system inside Nortel called bands, where people would be designated at a certain stature and they were paid according to the band they were in. And once you were in that band you would probably never be demoted. In many ways it resembled tenure. We went from that to one where it very much focused on somebody's contribution. As we started to contribution-rank our executive team, we found a lot of executives did not rank very well, and it reflected in their pay package pretty quick. Some decided to leave, and others we decided needed a push. So we ended up losing about a third of the executive team.

WSJ: In what areas has the right-angle turn not worked out so far?

ROTH: We have a long tradition of trying to get the best out of everybody as opposed to trying to get the best people. So our reluctance to deal with the bottom quartile of the population is the biggest challenge. This person's been with us for ten years, they really are in the bottom quartile of the company, but maybe I can make them a better person. . . . Will you ever get this person into the top half of our people? And the answer is, truthfully, no. Could you hire somebody who could be in the top half, and how long would it take? Maybe six weeks. So what do you do? That is very hard for us to come to grips with, but that's what we've got to do.

Stephen R. Hardis

CHAIRMAN

OF EATON

CORPORATION

Eaton Corp. is a lion of the Old Economy. Founded in 1911 to make truck axles, it has evolved into a major industrial manufacturer with $8.4 billion in sales last year and 63,000 employees in twenty-three countries. But no matter how much it earns or innovates, it still makes boring stuff—like electrical switches, truck parts, and other building blocks of the Old Economy. And as everyone knows, the future belongs to the New Economy's lithe gazelles, the Ciscos and the Amazons of the world.

Or does it?

In the view of Eaton chairman Stephen R. Hardis, companies in the so-called Old and New economies aren't really so different. In fact, they are inextricably tied and headed toward a common fate. As traditional ones rely more on advanced technology to squeeze out profits, they are starting to act more like their high-tech brethren. For example, luring knowledge workers has become crucial at Old Economy companies as they shift into the Internet age.

New Economy companies, meanwhile, are getting their own cold splash of reality. It turns out profits do matter. Great ideas still attract capital, but to survive over the longer run, start-ups are finding they have to learn to do some low-tech things better, like packing and shipping merchandise in time for Christmas.

Mr. Hardis sees the two economies converging. "What we really should be talking about is differentiating between opportunities that have elasticity of demand and those that don't," he said in a June 2000 interview with The Wall Street Journal.

WSJ: What can older companies learn from the New Economy companies?

HARDIS: We clearly have to shift our resources to areas where there is more elasticity of demand and therefore greater opportunity. The trap has been inertia: We spend a lot of money refining products. You can get to the point where you add something . . . just because your engineers find those to be exciting problems.

You can't sell more transmissions than you sell trucks. Once you get 100 percent of the market, no matter what you invest, it can't be a growth business. Now, if we add on truck transmission radar-based collision avoidance, that's new functionality. If I can get that down to a unit price of affordability, we can get that on most commercial vehicles and ultimately on faster cars. That's elasticity of demand.

So what is the lesson learned? Don't have your resources trapped in areas that are inherently zero-sum games with a very marginal return. Shift your resources into areas that build on your strengths.

WSJ: What do New Economy companies need to learn from the established companies?

HARDIS: I don't think anybody has even thought that, much less asked the question. . . . The dot-coms are different from many of the prior venture capital–type investments because they started out intellectually intensive as opposed to capital intensive. . . . But once they get big, they become capital intensive and they become very sensitive to how efficient they are relative to routine things like, what is your fill rate? What is your cost of logistics? Hey, what's your cost of real estate? How many months of burn rate do you have left if you can't do another equity offer?

I heard some guy on public radio a couple of weeks ago. He had a creative idea. "We have to sell this stuff for more than it costs, because we don't know when we go out with another equity offering." Isn't that terrific?

What can they learn? In the final analysis you have to run every element of the value chain very productively. That great creative idea may have been great in Day One, and it may have been great to get your business plan through and sell stock, but it will not assure that you can survive, particularly now that the market has started saying maybe the ability to generate cash and to earn does matter.

I am not one of the people who thinks electronic commerce is a fad. I think it is a game change. But it is among a series of game changes that we have seen since the start of the industrial revolution. It is the latest important game change.

Those who survive are going to be good at managing large capital requirements, large employment, and doing a lot of traditional infrastructure things well. What seemed dull is all of a sudden going to seem like an imperative to survive. I also think you will find a lot of people saying, "Gee, we need people who know how to manage scale." So you are going to see more people move from traditional industries.

WSJ: You liken talking about your stock on Wall Street to being a tour guide in Croatia. Do you see that attitude changing?

HARDIS: Put it this way: They are sending for brochures, but they ain't signing up for the bus tour. Aggressive growth markets sucked all the money out. Now you can't get a fundamental rally in more traditional equities until the money starts flowing back. And we haven't seen that.

WSJ: Does the traditional sector of the economy need an evangelist?

HARDIS: Individual enterprises do. I don't know if a sector does. . . . The stock market is such an imperfect measure of success. We need leadership that transcends all of the dissonance, [the] counterproductive feedback we are getting from this stock market. . . .

People talk about traditional industries as maintaining the status quo and new economies inventing. Well there is no defense of the status quo. If you are not changing, you are not winning. It is harder to change an established organization with an embedded culture—harder to change behavior and give up things people are familiar with—than it is to create a new strategy in terms of management. We need leadership that causes people to really believe that change is in their interest. And that is a very tough message.

WSJ: Much of that leadership role has been relegated to consultants. Is that a mistake?

HARDIS: If you outsource the intellectual task of shaping priorities and direction, you forfeit leadership. And too often, it's a way of copping out. Someone says: "I don't know what I am going to do, so I'll hire a consultant." . . . I think true leaders should always be willing to synthesize the best ideas in the society. . . . If you've got a particular area where you need to move quickly, yeah, bring in those resources. But you can't delegate leadership and be successful.

WSJ: Do you have a problem-solving technique that has stood the test of time?

HARDIS: I was a liberal arts major, which means you do a lot of reading, a lot of synthesizing. You try to synthesize a lot before you rush to judgment. . . . I don't believe in epiphanies, but you often get an insight somewhere that crystallizes something that's been bothering you.

WSJ: Can you give an example?

HARDIS: [I once accepted an invitation to attend one of those fund presentations in a hotel ballroom.] We didn't belong there, but we were sitting too close to the front to walk out. I felt trapped.

Then [the speaker] said something: "When we go into a developing country like a Malaysia or a Thailand or an Indonesia," he said, "we don't try to guess which PC maker is going to make it. We invest in cement and electric generation, because they're sure winners." . . . And I sat there and said, "You are putting down cement for roads, and the first thing on the roads is commercial vehicles—and that's Eaton. You are going to have generation on one side, and on the other side is going to be a circuit breaker—and that is Eaton." And I thought, "Why aren't we giving higher priority to the fact that our products are for the most part tied to infrastructure development? Are we really giving priority to these developing countries?" . . .

That led to a group within the company that was asked to go look at the data, look at the opportunities for our products, and come back with a report. And as happens sometimes when you're really lucky, they came back with specific data, specific recommendations, which led to a very conscious decision in 1995 to prioritize by product and by country where we had to go in terms of world growth. But the nickel went down when I heard that guy say: "We invest in concrete and electricity."

WSJ: What's the most critical part of your daily routine?

HARDIS: The most important thing I have to do is to be psychologically available. . . . A big mistake in a job like this is to get so scheduled and so intent on your own priorities that you are not flexible enough to respond to the unexpected issue, where someone will come on in and basically say, "There's a problem you should be aware of." Sometimes they are looking for you to legitimatize an action that they know they have to take. . . . Sometimes it is just helping them sort out the problem by asking the right questions.

WSJ: Is there a certain time you set aside for this sort of interaction?

HARDIS: Between five and six-thirty is the time when the white noise dies down, people feel more comfortable drifting in. . . . I also try very hard to use the lunches that aren't already scheduled to invite somebody from within the company to lunch.

WSJ: So you randomly pick somebody in the organization from time to time to have lunch with?

HARDIS: Typically, I'd do it that same day. . . . And I usually have my assistant make the call, so if they have another appointment, she can put them at ease and say, "That's fine." I am always afraid if I make the call, they will cancel something else because they will feel like it's bad not to accept.

WSJ: Is it hard to recruit people to work for a traditional company like Eaton?

HARDIS: Yes. We have a very good retention rate, if we can get them here, because we have a lot of qualities at Eaton that a certain group really values. This is a gross generalization, but I grew up in New York, so I am permitted. On the East Coast and the West Coast, sentences start first-person singular—"I," what's in it for me, my career. The Midwest is truly different—it's much more collegial. They like team sports. Are *we* winning? Some people like a company that does care about how you win, about team effort and staying power and caring about the community. Obviously, we're under pressure for costs, but we really try hard to be responsible.

WSJ: How much of the problem is the place itself—Cleveland?

HARDIS: It is hard to get people into Cleveland. . . . It's easier in May than it is February. But it's hard to get them to move, once they're here. Nobody went to business school daydreaming about a job offer from Eaton. They did about Cisco and Microsoft and Oracle. So we have a much tougher sell.

Jeff Bezos

FOUNDER
AND CHIEF
EXECUTIVE OF
AMAZON.COM, INC.

What to do? Your in-basket is jammed. Your phone is ring-ing. You're fifteen minutes late for the next meeting and an anxious-looking subordinate is demanding to talk "just for a minute." Some people might call that a crisis. Millions of managers call it typical.

Of all the top executives in America, few keep a pace as frenetic as Jeff Bezos, the founder and chief executive officer of Amazon.com Inc., the Seattle-based online merchant. His fast-growing company is packed with ambitious managers wanting his attention. Meanwhile, outsiders have redoubled their efforts to get at least a sliver of his time.

How does a CEO keep his or her week under control, in an age when Internet technology bombards us with more information than ever? In a 2000 interview, Mr. Bezos shared his strategies for time management—some of which are as provocative and untraditional as Amazon's retailing strategy.

WSJ: What do you do to avoid being completely deluged by e-mail?

BEZOS: It's easy to let the in-box side of your life overwhelm you, so you become a totally reactive person. . . . The only remedy I know of is to set aside some fraction of your time as your own. I use Tuesdays and Thursdays as my pro-active days, when I try not to schedule meetings. I let the other three days of the workweek be completely scheduled, meeting with different general managers in our businesses. That works pretty well for me. And I try to travel about a third of the time. If I travel much more than that, I lose my Tuesdays and Thursdays.

WSJ: Tell us some unusual things you've done on Tuesday or Thursday that paid off.

BEZOS: I've gone shopping in malls many times, just to see how stores are laid out.

I spend a lot of time on Tuesdays and Thursdays look-ing at our website. When I'm objective, I think it's by far the best e-commerce site out there. But when I look at it on Tuesdays and Thursdays, I see all these little things that make me cringe. That's important.

And I surf the Web regularly. A few weeks ago, a friend told me to look at a small e-commerce site, because he thought it had a good decision tree for buying fax machines. Unfortunately, it took me a couple days to follow up. When I got there, I saw a notice saying that the site had shut down. I didn't get there fast enough.

WSJ: Anything else?

BEZOS: I try to use Tuesdays and Thursdays to say thank you to people. I still don't do that nearly enough. It's a classic example of something that's never the most urgent thing to do. But it's actually very important, in a soft way, over a long period.

WSJ: You have 16.9 million users. How do you take their pulse? Do you use traditional focus groups, or does new technology open up fresh options?

BEZOS: Yes to everything. We've gotten more feedback in the last four years than most traditional companies have in forty years. We use it to improve our services. One simple— and very effective—thing we do is to e-mail a question to three thousand randomly selected customers. We might ask them: Besides the things already in our stores, what else would you like to see us sell? The responses can be incredibly interesting.

E-mail in general is a very useful feedback mechanism. That's because e-mail turns off the politeness gene in human beings. People are more willing to be rude and truthful by e-mail than they ever would be in person or over the phone. For a company, that's wonderful.

Focus groups are great for developing intuitions. But your total sample size is maybe twenty or twenty-five people. If you use that to answer questions, you're in great danger of making anecdotal conclusions.

WSJ: How much do you get involved in each new growth initiative at Amazon? Are you there to inspire people, scold them, or be the strategic big thinker?

BEZOS: I have a couple of roles. One is to make sure that people know that things that seem impossible often aren't. I'm well-suited for that, knowing that everything we've done at Amazon seemed impossible at the time. Also, I'm often encouraging people to go faster, even if it means a worse initial product. I want us to start learning. At a certain point, I step out of the way and let the work get done. Then I come back after the thing is already up on the website and suggest changes.

The point is, it's almost impossible to make an irrevocable mistake on the Web. The cost of trying to avoid mistakes would be huge in terms of reducing speed. So it's much better to get things done fast, and then fix them after the fact.

WSJ: How do you run a meeting when other people have intense technical knowledge that goes beyond yours? As you spend more time in general management, do you still know the technology well enough to know where to push the company?

BEZOS: This is an age-old problem. To begin with, probably you shouldn't be running that meeting. Somebody else should.

I think about this in hiring, because our business all comes down to people. My background is computer science, so it's easy for me to interview chief information officers and see if they really know what they're talking about. It would be much harder for me to evaluate a chief accounting officer. In fact, when I'm interviewing a senior job candidate, my biggest worry is how good they are at hiring. I spend at least half the interview on that.

WSJ: How do you work with your directors? Something tells me this isn't quite like U.S. Steel in the 1920s, with a long mahogany table and six-hour board meetings.

BEZOS: We're actually a little old-fashioned in this respect. There's nothing better than an in-person meeting. Nothing yet has replicated that, as far as I know. For quick inter-action, e-mail and phone are great. But for really getting into something, a physical meeting is much better. We laugh a lot at our board meetings—and we get a lot done. In our case, a lack of formality leads to a lot more activity.

WSJ: Almost every founder has a tough time knowing what to delegate. You used to do it all when you were a one-man company. Do you know when to pull back?

BEZOS: I used to sign all our checks for special-order books— and I worked so hard to get rid of that task. It got to be two hundred signatures a day. These were checks for all of twenty-five dollars apiece, and it became clear that if I didn't do something about it, I'd be doing nothing else. If you get to the point that you don't have any time to be proactive, it probably means you aren't delegating enough.

WSJ: Your stock price is down more than 25 percent since Christmas. Does that affect your decision-making, or are you oblivious to it?

BEZOS: "Oblivious" is too strong a word. But I believe Peter Lynch said that in the short term there's no correlation between stock price and great companies. In the long term there's a 100 percent correlation. So if you base your strategy on your short-term stock price, you're at the mercy of something you don't control. Watching the price on a daily basis will drive you crazy.

WSJ: You have this custom in December that every employee—including senior managers—helps pack goods in the warehouses or fields customer-service calls. Why is it part of the drill?

BEZOS: It's amazing how much you learn by doing something that's very close to customers, even for a brief period. . . . Working in one of our distribution centers, you understand that if a shipment doesn't go out on time, some child isn't going to have anything under the tree on December 25. That makes our purpose very real.

Five Lessons from Jeff Bezos on Time Management in a Wired World

1. Set aside Tuesdays and Thursdays as your own, without any regularly scheduled meetings.
2. Break your routines. Visit stores. Scrutinize your own website. Learn from unexpected places.
3. Work fast and fix small mistakes later. The only fatal error on the Web is being too slow.
4. Use e-mail aggressively to learn what customers think. They won't always be polite, but they will be candid.
5. Make time for thank-yous. That's never the most urgent task, but in the long run, it can be very important.

Gerd Wittkemper

EUROPEAN
CHAIRMAN OF
BOOZ ALLEN
& HAMILTON

Former U.S. vice president Al Gore's proposals for the "information-age town hall," where governments and citizens rely on the Internet for most of their interaction, turned the so-called e-government into a hot issue in the 2000 presidential campaign. The subject may not yet be as prominent on the European political scene, but that could change soon. Governments can generate substantial savings by delivering services over the Internet, while citizens would benefit from easier and quicker access to government organizations. Little wonder, then, that management consultants hope to apply some of their electronic-commerce know-how to the public sector. In a 2000 interview, Gerd Wittkemper, the European chairman of consulting firm Booz Allen &

Hamilton, discussed the topic with The Wall Street Journal Europe.

WSJ: For some time now, there's been a lot of talk about e-government. What's the basic idea?

WITTKEMPER: The transformations that have been initiated by the Internet do not only concern companies, they also affect citizens and the government. The government should be a role model in all of these developments. One would expect that taxes are being used in an efficient manner and that the government uses technology to do that. And the benefits of using the Internet for government services could be huge. German government expenditures, for example, are about 1.8 billion marks [920.3 million euros]. If you just save 1 percent, you've got almost 20 million marks saved.

WSJ: What are the different steps that a government can take?

WITTKEMPER: It's pretty similar to what companies are doing. It starts with pure information like introducing yourself, your goals, perhaps giving telephone numbers and so on. A second step would be turning the one-way street into a two-way street. Government agencies get in touch with citizens for anything from surveys to council meetings over the Internet. You could imagine legislation being shaped by citizens. And then there are referendums and elections, which gets you to the whole issue of the digital divide because not all citizens have a personal computer, so you'd have to have something like public Internet stations. A third step would be to conduct transactions over the Internet: The government uses the Internet to offer a better service, ranging from tax declarations to the issuing of identity cards. Additionally, the government can improve its relations with suppliers by doing procurement over the Internet.

WSJ: How would e-procurement work for governments?

WITTKEMPER: The Italian finance ministry, for example, has launched an e-procurement program that is being administered by a new centralized unit. Not every single ministry agency makes its own purchases, but all of them get together to make use of economies of scale. And technology can help to accelerate decision-making processes in procurement. Traditionally, individual government agencies would ask suppliers to make offers, then committees would meet to discuss them. Now the idea is that you establish electronic marketplaces for the same process. Business-to-business marketplaces already exist. It's up to governments to go the same route.

WSJ: So how far down the road are European governments?

WITTKEMPER: Generally, there seems to be a north-south difference. In Finland and in the U.K., for example, you can already file your tax declaration over the Internet. And some of the northern countries have created incentives for citizens to use these services. In the U.K., there's a concession for those who use the Internet for their tax declaration. It pays off for the government because it frees up tax agencies to focus on truly complex cases such as big companies. Germany, France, and Italy are also being pressured by industry to get ahead with e-government programs, whereas southern countries such as Portugal, Spain, and Greece are lagging behind.

WSJ: Why are consultants interested in this field?

WITTKEMPER: For Booz Allen & Hamilton this is a very
normal development since 40 percent of our worldwide
revenue comes from governments. But there's also a general consulting trend because other consulting firms
have noticed that there is a strong demand for advice on
e-government.

WSJ: But can governments even afford to pay the same rates
that companies pay for this kind of service?

WITTKEMPER: The business of consulting governments has
undergone a transformation. Ten years ago, government
organizations would bring in consultants for very specific
tasks such as making individual processes more efficient.
Now consultants help governments to restructure their
entire organizational structures. As a result, governments
are getting used to paying the same sums or almost the
same sums as companies.

WSJ: How does advising governments on e-business differ
from advising companies?

WITTKEMPER: Government organizations are run by politi-
cians who all have a say on the process, so you need to take
that process into account. In the private sector, you (as a
consultant) would establish a task force with managers,
write a report, make a presentation to the management
board, and then there will be a quick decision. Also, during the bidding process, the government has to guarantee
that all bidders are being given the same chance. So you
have a two-step process where the government first makes
sure that all the offers correspond to what is being asked
for and a second step where you negotiate about the price.

But in order to get faster in all of this, the government needs to be more flexible.

WSJ: How about employees? Do you see civil servants as more reluctant to implement some of these changes than employees in the private sector?

WITTKEMPER: You have to adjust organizational structures to these new challenges, and such restructuring has a deep impact on personnel. So if you're dealing with civil servants, you normally have to implement changes by training rather than relocating or laying off people. It's also very hard to employ financial incentives, since the use of bonuses is limited in the public sector. And again, all recommendations of consultants have to be fed into the democratic decision-making process and cannot be made by one chief executive on a single morning. So everything takes longer.

Part Five

Trendspotting

Tom Freston

CHIEF EXECUTIVE

OF MTV

NETWORKS

Teenagers and kids have perplexed marketers and their parents for years. So what do MTV Networks and its baby-boomer boss Tom Freston know that the rest of the youth-marketing pack doesn't?

As it enters its twenty-first year—the fifteenth with Mr. Freston as CEO—MTV Networks remains a trendsetter in the youth market with consistently fresh music, fashions, and personalities. Its children's channel, Nickelodeon, continues to rank among the country's most watched cable channels, and it has spawned licensed products ranging from Rugrats *personal computers to* Blue's Clues *pajamas.*

Even its VH1 music channel, a perennial ratings stepchild, has found a niche, developing popular new franchises like

Behind the Music *and* Divas Live *that have become cult hits with young adults.*

Mr. Freston, who began his career in advertising, links his success with young viewers to relentless market research, a dedicated staff of young employees who genuinely like their customers' tastes, and an understanding that the only thing constant in his business is change.

In a 2000 interview he talked about what it takes to stay clued in to the fickle youth market.

WSJ: How do you stay connected to the youth market?

FRESTON: We go after specialized audiences and we focus on that—which allows us to stay out of the fray of more mainstream television competition. . . . I think that if we can be totally connected with our viewers . . . and get inside their heads and get inside their closets, their CD collections, and translate that along with a lot of internal intuition into a product, everything else in our business will fall into place.

WSJ: How do you do that?

FRESTON: A major focus here is on . . . consumer research. . . . We are probably the preeminent researcher of kids, teens, and young adults. . . . Nickelodeon is for kids ages two to twelve or thirteen. And MTV . . . the core audience is eighteen to twenty-four.

We do hundreds of different types of research. . . . We actually in some cases put people under hypnosis. . . . We will videotape their lives. We do a lot of quantitative stuff. But coupled with that is having an employee staff and cul-

ture that is inherently interested in what we do. It has its
ear to the ground, has good instincts and a good sense
for . . . shifts in the wind.

While we stay focused [at] MTV on the teen and young-
adult audience, people pass through that demographic
rather quickly.

So just as you get accustomed to serving one group and
their particular attitudes or attributes . . . they have kind
of gone along. And a mistake is to move along with them.
There is a whole new generation coming in the pipeline
that is quite different.

WSJ: Do you go to clubs? Do you listen to that music?

FRESTON: Yes. I go to clubs. Long ago I turned over the
responsibility of actually picking the music on MTV. If it
was dependent on my taste, we would be out of business now. . . . We have people who really do go to the clubs
all the time with an eye for what is going on. Sort of an
early warning system for breaking trends and so forth. . . .
I will watch MTV and VH1 all the time, all day. And the
great thing about being . . . here in this building is I can
watch all our international feeds. I can watch MTV India,
or VH1 Germany. So I am a fan, but I am not picking the
music.

WSJ: Can you give us examples of how you find out what your
viewers want?

FRESTON: In the case of "TV Land" and "Nick at Nite,"
which is classic TV, we went out to Las Vegas . . . and we
hypnotized the young baby boomers and the older baby
boomers—people thirty-five to forty-five and forty-five to

fifty-five. . . . This is not something we do regularly, it isn't mainstream, but it is interesting. We played [these two groups] some old commercials and played them old TV shows [while they were under hypnosis] and asked them to remember what it was like watching TV when they were seven, when they were fourteen, when they were in their teens. . . . Because [some of what] we do is . . . take old shows and try and put a spin on them and make an environment that forges a connection.

WSJ: What do you see as the next trend after hip-hop and women stars?

FRESTON: The pendulum between rock-based music, which is lyrically driven, and rhythmic dance music has been going on a long time. Right now . . . we are in a rhythmic dance groove. And rock music . . . certainly appears to . . . be sleeping. . . . Hip-hop and rap music are king today and will probably remain so. . . . It is the only new thing since the advent of rock music. And apart from pure hip-hop and rap music . . . is the influence it has on other forms of music. You see hard rock/rap. You see R&B/rap. Or dance/hip-hop. Outside of, like, country music, it has . . . affected almost everything. . . . That trend is going to continue to grow. . . .

The days of the international superstar that we saw mostly from the Anglo-American music community in the seventies and eighties . . . has peaked as more and more countries have . . . their own popular music. They have their local stars who sing in their own language about things that are more relevant to them. . . . Domestic music, be it German, Japanese, Chinese, I think is going to be on the ascendancy.

wsj: It sounds as if you are not trying to take an American version of what is popular and implant it globally. You are trying to allow what is there already to emerge.

FRESTON: Yes. People talk a lot today about the increasing homogenization of the world. . . . That really isn't true. Kids today, outside the U.S. in particular . . . travel with two passports. They have the international passport . . . that plugs them into what is going on with their peers around the world. So when you talk about action movies, sports stars, certain music stars like a Mariah Carey, certain kinds of clothing and styles, there is a homogeneity. But while that trend is going on, they have their other passport that is about their local world, which increasingly is more important to them. We play into that.

wsj: What generation do you think will be most important to watch?

FRESTON: The twenty-five-plus audience is going to be more adventurous. . . . But I think all the big musical trends for the next ten to twenty years are going to probably come from this younger, new, very large . . . Generation Y. The oldest people [of Generation Y] are now seventeen years old. It is a generation bigger than the boomers. . . . They now are responsible for this boy-band pop music. . . . They have grown up in a life of affluence and good times, and their music reflects that. It is happy, party music. . . . And somewhere among them today is a Bob Dylan or a John Lennon and Paul McCartney, or a Marvin Gaye.

WSJ: How do you know that?

FRESTON: It seems inevitable. How are you going to have so many people with a generational consciousness about themselves who are so different and so enthralled in the new-media technology and such a force? When they get to be in their twenties and thirties, they are not going to be listening to Backstreet Boys. . . . They are going to have someone who is really talking about their lives.

WSJ: What trends do you think MTV has been responsible for?

FRESTON: Some trends MTV has been helpful to either start or promulgate would include . . . Nickelodeon. Sort of cutting-edge, young-adult animation. It never existed anywhere else. . . . I think it is fair to say that MTV, while it didn't invent rap and hip-hop, certainly . . . took it to . . . the mass American market. . . . That music and all the things that you attribute to it in terms of style and dress, we . . . put in people's living rooms.

WSJ: What marketers do you admire outside your own business?

FRESTON: We tend to think of the people who have been very successful in terms of branding: AOL, Apple Computer, Pepsi and Coke, Virgin [Atlantic Airways]. Sony PlayStation, I think, has been fantastic.

WSJ: How has your management style helped you reach the youth market?

FRESTON: We have tried to avoid the command, cult-of-personality type of company, which you see a lot of in the entertainment business. . . . If you want to have a creative, cutting-edge company, there has to be . . . bottom-up idea flow. . . .

WSJ: How do you encourage that?

FRESTON: We are decentralized. . . . We have an informal work culture. You want people to think it is a fun place to work. So many of the entertainment companies today, particularly with the megamedia conglomerates, have really become like factories. So I try to give this place a sense of smallness. We don't go around saying we are the biggest. . . . The idea is, this is still a boutique . . . where someone can make a difference.

WSJ: Has the fact that you came of age in the youth culture of the 1960s made you more attuned to today's youth market?

FRESTON: I wasn't a child of the sixties in the classic way. . . . I wasn't a hippie or a political radical. But I was there . . .

Five Lessons from Tom Freston on How to Capture the Elusive Teenager

1. Consumer research is key. Do as much as you can.
2. When a generation moves on, don't follow it. Focus on the next one coming up.
3. Develop a young staff and culture that are inherently interested in what you do.
4. Make your business a fun place to work where ideas flow from the bottom up.
5. Remember that Chinese, German, and American teens have different experiences. Cater to local tastes.

and the sixties in some ways were a prelude for the [pop culture] industry. In the sixties you got a sense that new things were possible. You got a sense that nonconformity was something not to be feared but something to be revered. . . . It was the first time there was a real sense of generational consciousness . . . and we basically built the business around that issue, around generational unity.

Emily Woods

CHIEF EXECUTIVE

OF J.CREW

*In 1983, Emily Woods entered her family's mail-order busi-
ness and, at age twenty-one, launched the J.Crew brand.
What began as a pioneering line of casual fashion, built on
affordable weathered chinos and simple crew-neck T-shirts,
is today a $700 million empire locked in fierce competition
with rivals including Banana Republic, American Eagle,
and Gap.*

*In fashion, as in an increasing number of other businesses,
innovation and imitation happen at warp speed. The game is
won by constantly creating a sense of the new and exciting.
As Ms. Woods expands her catalog, retail, and Internet operations and prepares to take J.Crew public, the chairman
explained how she keeps it all fresh.*

WSJ: When you started J.Crew, what was your vision?

WOODS: It was a lot about wanting to design and sell clothes
we couldn't find anywhere else. . . . A couple of the first
items that were off the charts when we put the company
on the map were, believe it or not, a solid, hundred-percent
cotton T-shirt with nothing written on it. Because at the
time T-shirts were really sport T's. And they had graphics
on them . . . or they were undershirts. . . . And the chino—
the button-fly, stonewashed, stone-colored chino—didn't
exist before we did it.

WSJ: What are some of the smartest bets you ever made?

WOODS: Mix-and-match swimwear was a big one. When we
first introduced bikinis, I think we were the first company
that introduced tops and bottoms that you could buy sep-
arately [by size]. This had always been an issue for me
growing up. . . . And cashmere . . . I think we have seen
that trend ahead of time. Eight or ten years ago, we got
into year-round cashmere for men and women . . . in
fifteen-plus colors.

WSJ: Is that because you, Emily Woods, like cashmere?

WOODS: I don't like cashmere, I am sort of obsessed with it. I
think 90 percent of my sweaters are cashmere. I have more
than I care to admit.

WSJ: Now there are a lot of competitors trying to grab different pieces of your business. How do you make sure J.Crew
continues to stand for something beyond what the others
offer?

WOODS: You can't go into any of those competitors and buy
for yourself everything from underwear to beach, vacation,

weekend, and go-to-work clothes. . . . I mean, there are competitors that are focusing on college customers. Or they are doing . . . casual weekend wear, and we have a part of the line that competes with that. There are competitors doing European, sophisticated fashion. . . . but there really isn't a competitor at our price point who competes across our breadth.

WSJ: What specifically sets J.Crew apart from competitors?

WOODS: First and foremost, we don't brand our clothes. So you are not walking around with "J.Crew" on your clothes. . . . We had a moment of trying logos [in fall '98], which I know I didn't want to do, shouldn't have done, and am glad it didn't work. . . .

Part of being real, I think, in a very simple sense to me, has always been we don't pretend to be an athletic organization, or gym club, or department at any time. . . . I think bold and sophisticated color is a big part of who we are . . . like fuchsia, stone, and mauve.

WSJ: Does the customer care if you call it fuchsia as opposed to hot pink?

WOODS: Hot pink doesn't sound very J.Crew. So there you go. We would do fuchsia and we wouldn't do hot pink. . . . I think those kinds of details make a difference in the overall brand perception, definitely.

WSJ: How do you figure out the next season's designs?

WOODS: It's mostly going back in time, as opposed to looking at what is current. Because what is current is less relevant to what you want to look like the next year. . . .

The designers are always gathering and editing, always

traveling . . . most importantly, to unexpected places, from Louisiana to Vegas to Greece to the International Museum of Umbrellas in Fiesole, outside Florence, looking for inspiration, new materials, fabrics, color in blown glass, texture in corrugated paper, architectural influences. . . .

For example, Ursula [Andress]'s bikini in *Dr. No*, Audrey Hepburn's style in *Wait Until Dark*, are important influences this year. It's about taking details, silhouettes, tailoring from the past, and modernizing them through so many new technologies in washes and finishes, in fabric like stretch, polar fleece, felt, silk-cashmere blends. . . .

There is a part of your closet that you want to move forward. And there is the part you want to stay the same, because it is such a part of your own personal style that it is never really going to change.

WSJ: As you get older, do you worry about staying in touch with trends?

WOODS: I think it is something to be very aware of. My own lifestyle is maybe younger than my years. Not being married, not having children . . . it's about staying out and about and looking, and reading the right materials and watching the right movies and listening to the right music. I just have to hang out with my ex [former husband, film producer Cary Woods] and I will be up on current trends, as he likes to remind me. . . . Plus, my current boyfriend is thirty.

WSJ: When did you stumble?

WOODS: Well, we have stumbled several times. . . . Two years ago or so, we did a somewhat slimmer pant for men. And it did so well in 90 percent of our stores that we went on a little bit of a too-mod track for men. So your own success can sometimes lead you in wrong directions. . . . Or we had just the right shade of chartreuse and then got into this green thing . . . with too many styles. A couple were great; a few more was too much. It didn't sell and hurt the look

---

Five Lessons from Emily Woods on Surviving in a Crowded Marketplace

1. Solve customers' problems: We were the first to mix and match bikini tops and bottoms by size. That was always an issue for me growing up.
2. Don't get carried away by one product's success. It can lead you astray. For instance, you don't want to be standing in your own manufacturing store a year later and looking at too much of a single color.
3. Don't shun classics—reinvent them. For instance, we've offered the traditional pea coat in new fabrics or colors for years.
4. Surround yourself with people you trust. . . . You can't run a business over a certain size and sign off on everything.
5. Stay current. . . . It's about reading the right materials and watching the right movies and listening to the right music and staying involved with younger people.

of the store. In this business those are some of the danger zones.

WSJ: Your father, Arthur Cinader, who retired as chairman in 1997, was perceived as being a very tough manager. Did that reputation rub off on you?

WOODS: I think Dad was tough in some uncomfortable ways, and I think some of the reputation may have rubbed off on me. . . . I know I am tough to work for. I have a very high standard that I hold myself to. I am proud of that. People here recognize that I work as hard or harder than anyone else.

WSJ: Which executives from other companies besides J.Crew do you admire?

WOODS: Ralph Lauren, for accomplishing a complete realization of his vision. Warren Buffett, for common sense, simplicity, understanding, integrity, and wisdom. Richard Branson, for leadership, innovation, and for having so much fun. And Jack Welch, for his corporate leadership qualities.

WSJ: What products do you admire?

WOODS: Apple, VW, and Absolut vodka, for brilliant marketing. Kiehl's [upscale beauty line], because of its quality and consistency. Ben & Jerry's, for quality, marketing, and fun. Ivory soap—can't live without it. And Krispy Kreme plain glazed, of course.

Part Six

Beating the Competition

Phil Condit

CHAIRMAN OF
THE BOEING COMPANY

How do you react when your competitor grabs headlines with a bold new initiative, prompting people to say your rival is taking the market lead?

That's a challenge Boeing Company chairman Phil Condit faces these days, as arch rival Airbus Industrie moves toward launching its proposed 650-seat A3XX jetliner—and takes the media spotlight. The plane, which Airbus says will cost $12 billion to develop, would supplant Boeing's 747-400 as the biggest passenger plane flying. Boeing is responding by offering a larger version of the 747, which the U.S. company says will cost $4 billion to develop. Airbus has garnered thirty-two orders for the A3XX and Boeing has yet to win a customer for the 747X, but it is still early in the race.

WSJ: To enter the new market for superjumbo jets, Boeing is offering a larger version of its current 747, while Airbus is offering the new A3XX. Some people say Boeing risks ceding this market segment to Airbus. Do you see this as a risk?

CONDIT: Competition is made up of the opportunity to be wrong. Just doing what your competitor does is probably the biggest opportunity to lose money. An example: Douglas and Lockheed both built tri-jets [in the 1960s] to the identical specs and just beat each other silly.

What you are trying to do is say, do you understand the market? Do you address it better than your competitor does? Our view is that this market is far better addressed by a derivative product that takes advantage of what we have than it is with an all-new airplane.

For us, today, there is no way we could economically do a brand-new airplane for this market. You cannot make the numbers work.

WSJ: Can Airbus make the numbers work?

CONDIT: There are people with suspicions that they can't. That isn't a claim I make. They get to worry about that.

WSJ: There is a lot of attention these days around Airbus, and one might get the impression that Airbus is driving the competition with Boeing. Is it?

CONDIT: I don't think so. Some of the things that we are doing now are clearly the result of where information technology is allowing us to go. In the U.S. economy in general, a few years ago people were wondering whether all this investment in information technology was ever going to pay off. And if you had been able to gain a couple of points of productivity, it was considered pretty good. We have just had months of 5-plus percent productivity gains, which are huge. So some of this is the result of being able to do it. It is an area we have been aggressively working on for about six years.

I am a great believer in competition. If you want people to be good, competition is a good thing. Without it, you get lazy—you don't push the boundaries. I would make the same argument for Airbus as I would for us. I think they have pushed us and we have pushed them. There is nothing wrong with that.

We have always had very healthy competition. There was never a period when we didn't. The players have changed.

WSJ: Boeing people have done some benchmarking against European companies. What have you found, and what can Boeing learn from European industry?

CONDIT: What you do in any benchmarking process is recognize that somewhere there is somebody with a better idea, and you look for them wherever they may be. What any good company needs to do is always be looking for good ideas—in your own industry and outside your industry.

There are things that a number of European companies do very, very well. I think there are some areas where the quality levels are very good.

The automobile industry is a great place for us to look. You can say airplanes are different because they do thousands of units and we do tens, as opposed to, how do they do right-hand and left-hand drive on the same production line and get the kind of efficiencies that they get? What does that mean for the variations that we do for customer customization? A lot of automakers learned to give customers what looks like flexibility by offering a number of different options and yet not have those drive the production line. How do you do that? We have tended to come at it much more from a customization standpoint as opposed to a multiple-options slant.

There is also clearly some very good industrial design in Europe.

WSJ: Boeing has been able to save significantly on its taxes through foreign sales corporations [FSCs], a tax shelter set up by the U.S. government that the World Trade Organization has ruled to be in violation of its rules. Last year alone, Boeing saved $230 million on taxes thanks to FSCs. What is the competitive impact on Boeing if FSC rules change?

CONDIT: It is the same thing that happens any time tax laws change or tax rates change.

Right now, the U.S. is trying to rewrite its tax laws to be WTO compliant.

Every country in the world has some sort of export incentives. Part of the issue is, how do you apply what we call in the U.S. tax equalization? How do you apply rules that are written based on value added in the same way you apply rules that are written based on income. Not everyone writes their tax rules the same way. Part of the WTO process is trying to find out, are these equivalent enough that it is okay? But almost everybody's got export support. In Europe, exporters get a refund on VAT, which is in effect an export subsidy. How do you balance that with the equalization that goes on?

Everybody on all sides of the issues is going to try to make their point as best they can. We live in a world where everybody's rules aren't exactly the same. Where are we trying to go? Overall, to a more common set of trade rules.

I have no worries about competing on a relatively level playing field.

Heinrich von Pierer

CEO OF

SIEMENS AG

Heinrich von Pierer, the chief executive officer of Germany's Siemens AG, is so fierce on the tennis court that such prominent opponents as German chancellor Gerhard Schroeder have given up trying to beat him. One story goes like this: During a game of doubles, the trim Mr. von Pierer was teamed up with a portly partner against Mr. Schroeder and another player. Frustrated at having fallen behind, Mr. von Pierer yelled at his teammate, "You have to hate your opponent!" before instructing him to simply stand still in a corner. Then Mr. von Pierer dashed back and forth across the court in a one-man show to take the set.

The contrast with Mr. von Pierer's image as CEO of the sprawling Siemens conglomerate couldn't be greater. A tiger on the tennis court, in managing the electronics and electrical-engineering giant he is a staunch defender of Germany's managerial model, which eschews autocracy in favor of consensus among bosses and workers. Analysts have criticized him for not being as tough as his U.S. counterpart, General Electric Co.'s Jack Welch, but Mr. von Pierer insists that in Germany, and Europe in general, brass-knuckle tactics won't get you far.

Indeed, Mr. von Pierer has something to show for his style. Although he has restructured the company during his eight years as CEO and shed more than seventy thousand jobs from a German workforce that now stands at around 180,000, the employees have never once launched a strike in protest. Siemens is to be listed on the New York Stock Exchange next month.

In a 2001 interview in Berlin, Mr. von Pierer talked about management, tennis, and the German economic model.

WSJ: What excites you about tennis?

VON PIERER: First of all, every sport is about the fighting spirit, about winning as much as possible and to lose as seldom as possible. You have to learn how to win and lose. Yes, you even have to learn how to win, how not to become arrogant, because concealed within each victory is the seed for the next defeat if you make a mistake. That's why one shouldn't get so terribly upset about losing, but rather shake it off and get back down to business.

In tennis, you are on your own, and it's important to prepare yourself well. Perhaps I play well because I'm always well prepared. Secondly, you have to be able to judge your opponent. I can tell after warming up for a few minutes where his weaknesses are, where his strengths are. And I know, of course, my own strengths and weaknesses and can adjust my game. And it's also about pursuing the right strategy. And in contrast to soccer, where you can be sure that it's over if five minutes before the end of the game you're behind 3–0, in tennis you still have a chance right up to the last ball. You have the chance to completely turn the game around.

WSJ: Deciding to take control of the game against Chancellor Schroeder also was a kind of management decision, no?

VON PIERER: That was a crisis! And then I said, "Stop being so friendly to your opponent. You have to hate your opponent for a while!"

WSJ: What's the lesson for management?

VON PIERER: You have to be a little aggressive sometimes and change your tactics. There's no point in playing the same ball over and over if you are literally running into a tennis wall. Then you have to say, "Now is the time for change."

WSJ: How would you compare your management philosophy for Siemens with that on the tennis court?

VON PIERER: . . . You can draw a lot of parallels. You have to demonstrate a certain mix of aggression and accommodation. In tennis, you'd say defensive. A sport can't only be made up of offense; you can do both and get to know your opponent better. And never underestimate him. That's something I learned in my days of playing tennis, that I've had to suffer bitter defeats because I underestimated my opponent. That doesn't happen to me anymore.

WSJ: If there's a benchmark manager in your industry, then it's Jack Welch. How do you feel about that?

VON PIERER: No one should be the benchmark a hundred percent. But I have to say that we have taken a lot from GE, from Jack Welch. And it wasn't so easy in a company like Siemens to tell people to look around and see what we can learn from others. One example is benchmarking. Today it's a part of our corporate culture.

Jack Welch visits every division twice a year and speaks to them for a whole day about management development. I do that, too. . . . [In one area] we launched an initiative that goes beyond GE. I've never heard Jack Welch talk about innovation. We spend a lot more money for innovation, on research and development. And then globalization. The great advantage of an American company is the large domestic market. I'd like to tell you that our home market is Europe, but we know it's not that easy. There's a big difference if I have a big integrated U.S. market or a fragmented European market.

WSJ: But you also say that you can't become a "Neutron Heinrich"?

VON PIERER: No, we have to do everything in the context of our European culture. If I had the nickname "Neutron Heinrich" . . . You know how the name evolved? Go through the factory like a neutron bomb, the walls remain standing and the people are gone. Well, with that nickname I wouldn't get very far here. I talk to the people about shareholder value and tell the people how important it is.

WSJ: How has managing Siemens changed over the years?

VON PIERER: The pressure from the capital markets is enormous. My predecessor was a magnificent man, but I don't think he knew the share price every day. The first thing we talked about when I came in this morning was the share price. Now in all of the big factory halls the first thing you see on the way in is the share price. The biggest changes are the significant influence of the capital markets and speed of decision-making.

WSJ: What aspects of the American business model would you say aren't worth adopting?

VON PIERER: The way one deals with people. One example is the German codetermination. Today I met with thirty representatives of works councils from all the operations in Berlin. In the Anglo-Saxon world, that always sounds so nice. But today the discussion focused on large drives, which we are restructuring. That has massive consequences. The works-council representative came and said, "We've taken a look at the master plan and we have suggestions from our plant, which is where our know-how lies, about where we could develop new business." That's great. That's also part of codetermination, that the people come with their own suggestions. Whether it's feasible, I can't say now. You have to understand, you come into a German board meeting and there you have ten capitalists and ten labor representatives. That demands different behavior.

WSJ: What kind of behavior? What's different?

VON PIERER: That you talk to the people; that you include them; that we make decisions dependent on a broader consensus.

WSJ: What's the significance of Siemens being listed on the New York Stock Exchange?

VON PIERER: We'll probably get a few more American share-holders, though now 10 percent of our shareholders are American. And I expect that the issue "acquisition currency" will play a role. But regardless of these things, I think that a global company like Siemens has to report its balance sheet according to U.S. GAAP [generally accepted accounting principles] because of investors who want us to be comparable with others. We have to accept that we have to do things the way they want. And that means that a company like Siemens, the most global in Germany, if not the world, that we play according to the rules of the global market, that we list in the U.S.

In the U.S. I'm very happy with business volume. We're coming close to $25 billion and more than ninety thousand people. We are a real American company. The one thing that is different in America is that we're not profitable enough.

WSJ: Is it a problem to manage a global company like Siemens when the management board is primarily made up of Germans?

VON PIERER: First of all, you have to see the top Siemens 100. That consists of the management of the business divisions and the regional companies. And today, at this level, we have hardly any Germans. In the U.S. you'll find few Germans, nor in Spain, France, or Latin America. There are locals everywhere. And these people play a significant role in our top leadership. We have sufficient global input in the company to assure that the German influence isn't overbearing.

WSJ: Two years ago, investors were calling for your head. What did that feel like?

VON PIERER: Oh, it wasn't quite that bad. It was more like "If things don't get better soon, then . . ." And it was at a time when I could see clearly that we had a more positive perspective. What I advise people in a crisis situation: Stay cool; for God's sake don't get swept up by any kind of nervousness. And in such a situation, clear leadership is required and we reacted accordingly; introduced our ten-point plan. [As in tennis,] sometimes you just have to show clear leadership.

Part Seven

Leading a
Successful
Turnaround or
Transition

Robert S. Miller

FORMER CHAIRMAN AND
CHIEF EXECUTIVE
OF FEDERAL-
MOGUL
CORPORATION

Robert S. "Steve" Miller, Jr., a celebrated corporate Mr. Fix-It, is cleaning up another mess. This time, it's a mess he helped create.

In September 2000, the turnaround specialist became interim chairman and chief executive of Federal-Mogul Corp., a big auto-parts supplier based in Southfield, Michigan, after its leader, Richard A. Snell, resigned. In assuming command, Mr. Miller cited the "enormous disappointment" caused by Federal-Mogul repeatedly missing investor expectations.

He played a similar turnaround role as the company's interim chief in 1996 while he and fellow directors mounted an outside search that landed Mr. Snell. The company had expanded beyond its basic business, engaged in aggressive accounting, and failed to fulfill Wall Street earnings estimates.

Federal-Mogul isn't Mr. Miller's first repeat rescue. He twice served as acting CEO of Waste Management, Inc. But he has also revived major companies on his first try. He was the main negotiator in the grueling 1980 loan bailout of Chrysler Corp. He rejoined Federal-Mogul on the day he finished advising Aetna, Inc., after the February departure of CEO Richard L. Huber, who had come under intense investor pressure over Aetna's low share price. Mr. Miller "is a very clear thinker and very unbiased," which helps "when you're trying to get your arms around a [difficult] situation," Aetna chairman William Donaldson says.

What does it take to lead a turnaround? Why do the best business doctors sometimes stumble? Mr. Miller, a tall and easygoing executive, tackled these issues during a 2000 Wall Street Journal interview hours after he addressed hundreds of anxious Federal-Mogul employees to calmly refute false rumors of a possible bankruptcy-court filing.

wsj: What did you learn about turnarounds from your Chrysler experience?

MILLER: . . . We had a problem with some Canadian banks. They were squirreling some of the money. . . . Well, pretty soon the European and American banks found out what the Canadian banks were doing. They were absolutely furious that we hadn't told them. What I learned right there in a very heated evening's discussion was, the only thing you've got to sell is your own personal credibility.

And when you have a point you need to win, they will believe you if you have been honest with them when things aren't what they want to hear. . . . Good or bad, tell them exactly the way it is. Tell them what you are hoping to accomplish. If they believe in you, then they will give you running room to do it.

WSJ: Should you tell the truth to everybody involved?

MILLER: Tell everyone the truth. That was a big part of this morning's meeting with our employees. They are all scared to death. . . . Should we talk about the bankruptcy word? . . . They are all around the water cooler talking about it. You better talk about it in very frank and candid terms. . . . So that is rule number one: Play it straight.

WSJ: What other rules have nine turnaround experiences in twenty years taught you?

MILLER: You need to make decisions. Don't study things to death. Most of the things that need to be done will be plainly obvious. . . .

WSJ: What should be rule number three?

MILLER: Listen to the customer. Your customers are usually more perceptive than you are about what you need to do with your company. . . .

WSJ: Should lesson number four be, take the pulse of employee morale?

MILLER: . . . One of the things I like to do at each location is go eat in the cafeteria. We don't even have an executive dining room here anymore. . . . But even by choice, the way I prefer to do it is go to the cafeteria and sit down with three people at a table for four . . . and just ask them,

"How is it going?" You can really learn a lot. . . . You give people a chance to say what's bothering them about their activity, they say it. Some of the things may not be practical or maybe we can't deal with them. But at least people are willing to speak up. . . .

WSJ: As part of your pulse-taking here, did you check into sales of corporate-logo products?

MILLER: If I can have one measure of how a company is doing, it is to go to the store where the company-logo gear is sold. Find out how many people really want to wear a Federal-Mogul jacket around their town.

This is one [lesson] from Aetna. . . . Aetna U.S. Health-care was under a lot of fire, as all HMOs have been of late. People were afraid in their neighborhood to admit that they worked for Aetna because they thought they were going to get a whole bunch of health-care complaints. . . . My sense was that people did not want to advertise they worked for Aetna. It would just get them into hot water. Fortunately, the average public is not mad at Federal-Mogul. . . .

WSJ: I understand you also invited Federal-Mogul people to e-mail you.

MILLER: I have personally answered them at least with, "Thanks for your crazy idea," if not a more elaborate answer. Got one two days ago from a fellow I [had] never met. But he had some ideas about how to deal with the aftermarket. . . . I will sit down with this fellow and talk more fully about his ideas. . . .

I spent most of my preschool years and all of my summers and vacations with my grandfather on the southern

Oregon coast in a town called Bandon. My granddad had a sawmill. . . . My grandparents' house was a little house out on the dock right next to the sawmill. . . . I think of that as the real world. That's where things are made that matter to us as Americans. Things that add to our standard of living.

WSJ: What's the relevance to a turnaround?

MILLER: Because that is what it is about. If this was just a slugfest between some bankers and stockholders, I wouldn't bother with it. This is about real people who have jobs and families and their standard of living. If we fail as a company, all of their hopes and dreams will be dashed. . . . Moreover, what they are producing is important to all of our standards of living. . . .

WSJ: Is the fifth turnaround lesson the need to exude calm confidence when everyone else is hysterical?

MILLER: I don't see calmness as the objective so much as just balanced realism. . . . A lot of these companies I get involved in have never been in a crisis. When one hits, they are totally destabilized and they don't know how to deal with it. . . .

WSJ: Is acting confident just as important as offering balanced realism?

MILLER: Confidence helps if in fact there is a business case to be made that, yes, we can work our way through this. I passionately believe that to be the case here with Federal-Mogul. . . . But it is not calmness for calmness's sake. It is calmness because I think it is merited here. . . . We have a job to do, and if we do it, this will all work out just fine.

WSJ: Did I miss any rules?

MILLER: The only other rule I have found is you don't have to fire the losing team in order to make [the company] a winner. . . . I call the CEO the coach. . . .

Do you have to go three or four layers down in management and blow everybody away and start over? The answer is no. Most of the people in these companies are quite capable of doing great work. . . .

WSJ: What thrill do you get from refloating corporate *Titanics*?

MILLER: Well, this is not something I had planned on when I got out of school. . . . My first real turnaround experience was when I left Ford [Motor Co.] in late '79 and came to Chrysler as it was going through its darkest hours. . . . [I] developed a real passion for saving a great American institution. . . . I used to wake up at five o'clock every morning in a cold sweat, worried that if I screwed up that day I could put half a million Americans out of work. It was just incredible pressure. By the same token, the thrill of getting it done . . . right and seeing how well Chrysler did in the years after that, it was a source of great pride. . . .

WSJ: In February [2000], you left an attempted turnaround of Reliance Group Holdings, Inc., with some bruises. Why did you step into such a deeply troubled business?

MILLER: . . . I went in with the title of president. I reported to the chairman and chief executive officer, Saul Steinberg, who was also the largest holder in the place. . . . I probably did underestimate the financial issues the company faced. . . . I can't say whether or not anything could have been done to come to a happier outcome than what has transpired. . . . It is very hard to write new insurance policies when the rating agencies are raising questions about your survival. That's just an inordinate marketing challenge. . . . The answer is that not every company can be salvaged.

WSJ: With Federal-Mogul's next permanent CEO likely to be picked by the end of January, will this be your last turnaround?

MILLER: This is my last turnaround. I have made that statement five jobs in a row.

(In September 2001, the Bethlehem Steel Corporation announced that it had hired Mr. Miller as its chairman and chief executive.)

Leslie Wexner

FOUNDER OF THE

LIMITED, INC.

Leslie Wexner opened the first Limited clothing store in 1963 in an Ohio shopping center. By the 1980s, The Limited, Inc., would grow into an empire of thousands of specialty stores sporting some of the best-known brands in shopping malls, including Express, Structure, Victoria's Secret, and Abercrombie & Fitch.

But by 1993, the company was running out of steam, out-maneuvered by nimbler competitors such as Gap Inc., J.Crew Group, Inc., and even department stores. For much of the decade, the retailer's growth chilled and earnings sputtered as its women's apparel stores floundered, losing their fashion direction and customers.

*With many investors giving up on The Limited, Mr. Wexner
began a long, personal crusade to change both his own management style and the company's internal structure. He met
with visionary leaders from inside and outside retailing, con-
sulted management experts on how to reconfigure operations,
and eventually began spending less time picking sweaters
and more time attending to the company's executive ranks.*

*The Limited adopted a centralized organizational struc-
ture, including a corporate "brain trust" of executives to over-
see design, marketing, and distribution across the company's
nearly five thousand stores. Now the nine retail brands are
encouraged to work together, sharing information and holding monthly meetings of divisional heads who had been fierce
sibling rivals under the old structure.*

*The makeover's results are beginning to show. The chains
are back to posting consistent gains in monthly same-store
sales, and The Limited's stock is now trading near its all-time
high. In a 2000 interview, Mr. Wexner spoke with us about his
seven-year journey.*

WSJ: As The Limited has grown from a single store to a retailing giant, how has your role as chairman and chief executive evolved?

WEXNER: I was an entrepreneur. . . . You start with one store
and you do all the jobs in the store, and then you have two
stores, and then ten stores, and then fifty and one hundred. . . . I think the second phase of the business was repli-
cating, creating other businesses and making acquisitions.
We were kind of a venture-capital company in hindsight.

WSJ: You were an incubator for retailers?

WEXNER: Yes. And in a way . . . too prolific. . . . [I was] running around, I don't think effectively leading the business. . . . [I was] spread so thin. And without a . . . functioning center of the business. So in hindsight, we weren't a very good venture-capital company.

WSJ: Looking back, what went wrong at The Limited?

WEXNER: I think what went wrong was the . . . entrepreneurial style wasn't working. The business had outgrown that in terms of complexity. Working harder at the specialty store format wasn't the way.

Leading brands is different from being an entrepreneur. . . . It was about looking at how the business was organized. . . . Are we a large group of specialty stores or are we . . . a family of brands?

WSJ: What does a family of brands mean?

WEXNER: The reason I like that [term] is that I like the association of family, in terms of relationships. I think what it really speaks to is that it is a team. Everyone in the business has to work together as a team. It speaks to how you think about sharing ideas.

WSJ: Where do you get your ideas?

WEXNER: I think it happens on a subconscious level. It is very important that I try to go to Europe at least four times a year and travel the stores. I look at magazines and shopping centers just to get input. So I can see things and put them together in ways that I can understand.

The only person who comes close to understanding that pattern is my wife. We were decorating something in the house, and I said, "Wouldn't it be great to put this shade of yellow with this shade of blue for this room?" She said, "Why do you pick that?" I said, "I don't know. You tell me about the room, and I just had this creative idea."

She kind of interrogated me about it: "You don't know where that idea came from?" I said, "It is out of my imagination." She said, "You were in Venice or Milan walking down the street and saw a bowl that I commented about: 'What an unusual combination of colors, that yellow and that blue.'" And my wife had complete recall, photographic memory. She repeated the conversation we were having that I had completely forgotten about. . . .

I just think it is out of pure imagination. And I also know that if you give me a blank piece of paper, I don't do well.

WSJ: What was the lowest point for you personally through the turnaround?

WEXNER: I think the toughest part was . . . to realize that you had a set of skills that got you so far, and to really look in the mirror and say, "That was great, but what's next?"

This is like you are a professional golfer. You really understand golf. And one day you look in the mirror and you recognize that nobody really cares about professional golf. You have to now be a football player. Well, golfers don't look like football players. And as an adult you are going to have to learn a new sport. . . . It was a tough moment.

WSJ: What brought you to the realization?

WEXNER: . . . It had something to do with meeting with [General Electric Co. chairman and chief executive] Jack Welch and [former PepsiCo, Inc., chairman and chief executive] Wayne Calloway. . . . I would try to go out and see other people, see what they were thinking and what they were doing.

I became pretty well acquainted with [Wal-Mart Stores, Inc., founder] Sam Walton. Sam had asked me to be on their board, which is one of the sillier mistakes I made— I didn't accept. I didn't want to take the time from my business.

When I talked with Calloway, I asked him how he spent his time. And he said that he probably spent . . . 40 percent or 50 percent of his time on people. To me, it was startling. I like people, but I am busy picking sweaters, visiting stores, doing things. How do you find that much time?

And he said, because the talent in the organization is the most important asset that you have. . . . Basically he saw himself as the goalie or the guardian, where he was the last set of eyes. He said no one in the enterprise with PepsiCo could be promoted to an officer. . . . that he didn't know.

I thought that was astonishing. Because our practice essentially was, I was responsible for the CEOs [of each division] and the CEOs were responsible for their own organizations.

And then I came back and I decided that I would test it. I said no promotions, no hires at officer level, internal promotions or internal hires. . . . That I wanted to meet candidates [first].

WSJ: And has it worked out?

WEXNER: It works. . . . And it has forced a discipline on the business. . . . I began to see myself as the chief personnel officer.

WSJ: What things are you looking for when you meet someone?

WEXNER: Do they know their job? The second thing I look for is, are they whole people?

Do they have balanced lives? Are they normal? Do they care about the community? . . . [Maybe] somebody said this person was just the brightest whatever in the world, but they are a workaholic. They get to work at seven and they go home at midnight. They don't have a life.

I am much more comfortable building an organization that sustains itself with people who have full lives. Their life doesn't have to be my life. I married late in life, and I have young kids. Some people are single, and some people choose different lifestyles. But they have whole lives.

What I look for thirdly is a sense of true responsibility for the people that they are working with. That they not only say it, but they demonstrate that they really do care about the other people they work with. You can't fake that.

WSJ: In recent years you've spoken with chief executives from many other industries. Who are some of them that you admire and why?

WEXNER: Clearly I admire Jack Welch, Wayne Calloway, Sam Walton.

I find there is a great similarity between fashion brands and the movie business. What fascinates me about a Martin Scorsese or a Steven Spielberg—I spent some time with both of them—is they can manage incredibly creative people. . . .

In the movies you have an enormous group of creative people. Everybody is creative. Directors are creative, producers are creative, the set directors are creative, the actors are creative, the costume designer is creative, the screenwriters are creative.

From a business organization point of view, the [question is], how do you bring all this creative talent together and make one movie? I went out to watch Spielberg, just to see. Because our industry sees itself as creative—and it is.

All these creative people get together and they make one movie. . . . And they can pretty consistently make good movies. How do they bring all that creative talent together and not explode? Basically it is really a lesson in simple points of coaching and alignment. There is a lot of communication. Everybody remembers every day what the movie is, and there is a way for the creative talent to feedback. I think looking at that industry was very insightful to me. . . .

[Fashion] designers are people who can walk in the room and say, "Pink!" and then cry and leave. The fact is that creative people can work together. They can partner and can team. . . . I'm completely fascinated with guys who make movies.

WSJ: What is the most important piece of advice you would give to other managers?

WEXNER: The best advice I got when I was starting the business [was from] my marketing professor at Ohio State. . . . He said that change is a habit and you have to get in the

habit of it. . . . And if you don't, you will find yourself losing the ability . . . just like physical skills. Keep your men-
tal muscle loose. You have to keep stretching.

WSJ: Which brands in particular at The Limited are you tar-
geting for improvement in the next six months?

WEXNER: Express is a top priority. Sales in the first quarter
were the best in the brand's history. We are in a fashion
cycle that is particularly well suited for Express.

WSJ: What is the biggest risk facing The Limited over the next
six months?

WEXNER: Believing that [the progress] is a fait accompli.
We've made significant progress, but there's a lot more
hard work to be done. We've embarked on systematic
change that will never end.

H. Lee Scott

CHIEF EXECUTIVE
OFFICER OF
WAL-MART
STORES, INC.

Passing the torch is one of the most challenging maneuvers in corporate America. In the past year, a number of companies fumbled the transfer, ultimately pushing out relatively new chief executives at the Procter & Gamble Company, Mattel, Inc., and Coca-Cola Co.

Wal-Mart Stores, Inc., the world's largest retailer, has had to make the move twice—when founder and retailing legend Sam Walton turned leadership over to David Glass in February 1988, and in January 2000, when Mr. Glass handed the top job to H. Lee Scott.

To make the change, Mr. Glass began planning for the succession more than five years ago. When he realized that no one in the company had a broad enough background to step easily into the top job, he began moving potential candidates into jobs for which they had little prior experience.

Mr. Scott, for example, had spent sixteen years in Wal-Mart's logistics operation, in which position he began as assistant director of the trucking fleet. He became Wal-Mart's top merchant, where he helped to increase sales while reducing inventory.

As Mr. Walton did before him, Mr. Glass elected to stay on in an advisory capacity after he stepped down as CEO to help Mr. Scott's transition. "People accepted me, because Sam showed he was supportive of my new role," Mr. Glass says. Still, Mr. Glass worried he would have trouble letting go, a mistake he has seen other corporate leaders make.

"I had to learn how not to make decisions," he says. "Lee and Tom [Coughlin, president of the Wal-Mart stores unit] made it easy for me. They solicited my opinion, used me as a sounding board, and felt comfortable disagreeing with me. It couldn't have worked out better."

Although the company's growth has fallen to its lowest pace in five years amid a softening economy, Wal-Mart, with revenue of $191 billion in 2000, has grown enough to overtake General Motors Corp. and become the world's second-largest corporation, behind Exxon Mobil Corp.

WSJ: What do you see as the biggest succession pitfalls other major companies have encountered, and how has Wal-Mart managed to avoid them?

SCOTT: I have only read about other successions, so I don't have any inside knowledge. But I think I can tell you why ours worked. First of all, [former Chief Operating Officer]

Don Soderquist, David Glass, and [Chairman] Rob Walton did a very nice job early on getting the executive group exposed to the board of directors. A lot of people don't talk about that, but one of the things [for] a new CEO is understanding and developing that relationship with the board so we understand what the expectations from the board are.

Second, we work in a company that is not ego-driven. It is driven by the customers' and associates' needs and not by the individual person who is CEO. Sam was probably as dynamic as anyone you will ever meet, but he never made the company revolve around him. So I think there is a different expectation when you come into this job. People don't look to you to have this huge ego and this CEO stature and image. I don't feel like now that I have this job, I have to become someone different.

Third, because we share so much information and this is such a centralized company in so many ways, you have a lot of common knowledge and knowledge across different business segments. Even if you haven't worked specifically in those segments, the learning curve as you move up in the organization is not as steep as you would think in a company this large.

WSJ: How did you decide how to handle the transition?

SCOTT: When David Glass, Rob Walton, and I sat down, we arrived together at the right way to do the transition. It was a partnership. It wasn't one of those things where someone called you in the office and said, "On this date we're going to do this." It was, "Here's what we are thinking about. Here's what we would like to accomplish. What do you want to accomplish? What would serve you?" We just worked it out, the three of us, with David setting the tone. It was just a very open and honest discussion from the very start. That was the most important.

WSJ: What was the plan?

SCOTT: We discussed the advantages of David staying on. We didn't talk about David staying on a year, but staying on as long as David felt good about staying. We talked about the difficulties. One day you're the CEO, one day you aren't. Life changes. One day I'm not the CEO, and the next day I am, and I'm in the same meeting with David Glass. We talked about those things before they ever occurred, and if we had an issue, how he and I would react. I pride myself on having a direct communication style. So I had no problem sitting with David telling him where the impediments might be. Nor did he have a difficult time telling me where the stumbling points might be.

WSJ: How does your leadership style differ from that of Sam Walton and David Glass?

SCOTT: I'm probably entering into a time [in which] the company is so much larger, being able to have the personal relationships that I would like to have at the store level, especially in the U.S., is just not possible. . . . I am trying to travel more internationally. I'm spending more time with the Sam's Club group. I probably have a little different focus than David had. That's natural. I'm certainly not trying to disregard anything domestically, but I understand that we have to make tremendous progress internationally if we want to grow at the rate our shareholders deserve to have the company grow.

WSJ: Have you made any mistakes?

SCOTT: The biggest mistake I made is not controlling my schedule. I was not prepared for the demands on my time—internally and externally. This week, I was in Miami visiting stores. I returned Monday evening to do the earnings release, then left for Mexico City, where I had a meeting Tuesday morning. I flew to San Francisco Tuesday afternoon for a meeting. Wednesday morning I was back in Bentonville [Arkansas], where I had a meeting with the vice mayor of Shanghai, China. In the afternoon, I flew to Little Rock to meet with senators and representatives of the state legislature. . . . I'm still trying to sort through this. I have to make sure I am in the stores and make sure I understand what is going on with the business.

WSJ: What is the single most important thing you've learned as CEO?

SCOTT: This job of CEO has much more responsibility than it does power. I'm not sure everyone gets it. I think they believe when you become CEO you simply can dictate and things will happen. But the truth is, you are so far away from it that it is through the influence of people that you cause things to occur.

Contributors

JACK WELCH

"How GE's Chief Rates and Spurs His Employees," by Carol Hymowitz and Matt Murray. *The Wall Street Journal.* 06/21/1999.

STEVE BALLMER

"Keeping On Course in a Crisis: Microsoft CEO Stresses Need to Simplify Goals, Heed Key Employees' Concerns," by Rebecca Buckman. *The Wall Street Journal.* 06/09/2000.

JOHN CHAMBERS

"How to Drive an Express Train—At Fast-Moving Cisco, CEO Says: Put Customers First, View Rivals As 'Good Guys,' " by Scott Thurm. *The Wall Street Journal.* 06/01/2000.

JUERGEN SCHREMPP

"Management: Making 'Digital' Decisions—DaimlerChrysler Chief Explains His Tough Calls," by Robert L. Simison and Scott Miller. *The Wall Street Journal.* 09/24/1999.

SANFORD I. WEILL

"Management: Recipe for a Deal: Do It Fast—Citigroup's Weill, an M&A Vet, Offers Some Tips," by Matt Murray and Paul Beckett. *The Wall Street Journal.* 08/10/1999.

DANIEL VASELLA

"Novartis Sizes Up Formula for Changes—CEO Tries to Mix Qualities of Big, Small Firms—Vasella Prizes Nimble, Efficient Operations," by Vanessa Fuhrmans and Frederick Kempe. *The Wall Street Journal.* 01/30/2001.

TINA BROWN

"Finding the 'Seduction Point'—How an Editor Grabs Attention in a Media Crowd," by Wendy Bounds and Carol Hymowitz. *The Wall Street Journal.* 07/26/1999.

IAN SCHRAGER

"The Nightly Balancing Act—Hotelier Ian Schrager Seeks the Perfect Guest Mix; Who's a Super Royal VIP?" by Wendy Bounds. *The Wall Street Journal.* 08/17/2000.

KEVIN J. ROBERTS

"Bringing Love to the Internet—Saatchi Chief Says Online Ads Have the Power to Change an 'Antisocial' Medium," by Suein L. Hwang. *The Wall Street Journal.* 05/18/2000.

MICHAEL DELL

"Get Into Gear Online!—PC Whiz Advises Auto Makers Web Is Best Venue to Handle Suppliers, Serve Customers," by Gary McWilliams and Joseph B. White. *The Wall Street Journal.* 12/01/1999.

JOHN ROTH

"Buying Into the New Economy—CEO Uses Acquisitions to Turn Nortel into a Huge Player in Technology for the Web," by Mark Heinzl. *The Wall Street Journal.* 07/25/2000.

STEPHEN R. HARDIS

"When Economies Converge—Game May Have Changed, but Eaton Chairman Says Old Industry Still Matters," by Timothy Aeppel and Clare Ansberry. *The Wall Street Journal.* 06/22/2000.

JEFF BEZOS

"Taming the Out-of-Control In-Box—For Amazon.com's Chief, The Secret Is Two Days for Strolling and Surfing," by George Anders. *The Wall Street Journal.* 02/04/2000.

GERD WITTKEMPER

"E-Business Moves into Government—Management Consultants Advise Europe's Civil Servants on Net Virtues—Getting in Electronic Touch with Citizens," by Konstantin Richter. *The Wall Street Journal.* 09/06/2000.

TOM FRESTON

"How MTV Stays Tuned In to Teens—CEO Recommends Hiring Staff That Appreciates Kids' Tastes and Doing Lots of Research," by Sally Beatty and Carol Hymowitz. *The Wall Street Journal.* 03/21/2000.

EMILY WOODS

"The Secret of Ursula Andress's Bikini—In a Battle to Be Forever New, J.Crew Chief Gets Her Ideas from Unexpected Places," by

Wendy Bounds and Rebecca Quick. *The Wall Street Journal.* 11/10/1999.

PHIL CONDIT

"Boeing Stays True to 747 Line—U.S. Plane Maker's Chairman Won't Alter Strategy with Airbus—Condit Says Economics Argue Against New Jetliner Model," by Daniel Michaels. *The Wall Street Journal.* 10/13/2000.

HEINRICH VON PIERER

"Goal Is Game, Set, and Match—Siemens' CEO Applies Tactics of Tennis to Management; Rules of Winning, Losing," by William Boston and Frederick Kempe. *The Wall Street Journal.* 02/02/2001.

ROBERT S. MILLER

"Tips from a Turnaround Specialist—Miller, Now at Federal-Mogul, Effects Corporate Revivals with Tell-It-Like-It-Is Style," by Joann S. Lublin. *The Wall Street Journal.* 12/27/2000.

LESLIE WEXNER

"A Makeover That Began at the Top—The Road from Entrepreneur to Modern Manager Was Rough for Limited Founder," by Rebecca Quick. *The Wall Street Journal.* 05/25/2000.

H. LEE SCOTT

"How Wal-Mart Transfers Power—Prior CEO's Careful Planning and Advice Helped Scott; So Did Exposure to Board," by Ann Zimmerman. *The Wall Street Journal.* 03/27/2001.